RESOURCE

GW00546956

on or before

NEW HORIZONS

science

Key stage 3

CAMBRIDGE

Project Development Team

Jim Hudson
General Adviser (Science)

Jon Sargent
Former Advisory Teacher

Wendy Jeffery
Chichester High School for Girls
Former Advisory Teacher and
Key Stage 3 Co-ordinator

Authors

Chris Brown

Paul Butler

David Carrington

Sam Ellis

Published by the Press Syndicate of the
University of Cambridge
The Pitt Building, Trumpington Street,
Cambridge CB2 1RP
40 West 20th Street, New York, NY 10011-4211, USA
10 Stamford Road, Oakleigh, Melbourne 3166, Australia

First published 1995

Printed in Great Britain at the University Press, Cambridge

A catalogue record for this book is available from the British Library

ISBN 0 521 39792 8

Photographic credits
Front cover tl: All Sport Ltd; tr, Dr Jeremy Burgess/ Science Photo Library; br, ZEFA

6 BIPM, Paris; 8*tr* Graham Portlock; 9*t* MEPL; 10 The Boots Company plc; 11 Science Photo Library/ David Scharf; 13 Environmental Picture Library/ Steve Morgan; 16*l* Dept. of Clinical Radiology, Salisbury District Hospital/ Science Photo Library; 16*r* Science Photo Library/ Chris Priest & Mark Clarke; 17*t* CNRI/ Science Photo Library; 17*b* Alexander Tsiaras/ Science Photo Library; 18*l* Zefa/ Rosmarie Pierer; 20*t* MEPL; 25*b* Proff Motta, Corner & Nottola/ University 'La Sapienza'/ Science Photo Library; 26*tr*, 27*tl* NHPA/ M.I. Walker; 28*t* NASA/ Science Photo Library; 28*c* Ford Motor Company; 28*b* All Sport Ltd/ David Cannon; 29 Science Photo Library/ A.B. Dowsett; 30*b* Science Photo Library/ James Stevenson; 32*t* MEPL; 33*t* Ann Ronan Picture Library/ E.P. Goldschmidt & Co Ltd; 34*bl* MEPL; 36/ 37, 38*bl* Graham Portlock; 39*t* ZEFA/ J Pfaff; 39*b* Golden Gate Bridge Highway & Transportation District; 40*b* Oxford Scientific Films/ Stan Osolinski; NHPA/ Stephen Dalton;46*r* Science Photo Library/ Tony Craddock; 48*r* ZEFA; 49 MEPL; 51*b* Science Photo Library/ Simon Fraser; 52*bl* Science Photo Library/ Martin Bond; 56*bl* NHPA/ David Woodfall; 58 Environmental Picture Library/ Philip Carr; 61*bl* Quadrant Picture Library; 61*tr* NHPA/ Henry Ausloos; 62*tl* Planet Earth Pictures/ Geoff du Feu; 62*tr* NHPA/ John Shaw; 62*bl* NHPA/ Peter Parks; 63*bl* NHPA/ Norbert Wu; 63*tr* NHPA/ Stephen Dalton; 64/ 65 Image Select; 65, 66*t* MEPL; 67*tr* NHPA/ Gerard Lacz; 67*bl* Planet Earth Pictures/ Wayne Harris; 68, 69 MEPL; 70 National Medical Slide Bank/ Wellcome; 71*t* Science Photo Library/ Biophoto Associates; 71*b* Jackie Lewin, Royal Free Hospital; 73*l* John Frost Newspapers; 73*r* Science Photo Library/ Proff. P.M. Motta; 74/ 75 John Frost Newspapers; 77*tr* MEPL; 78 The Cavendish Laboratory, University of Cambridge; 79*t*, 79*b* MEPL; 81 The Cavendish Laboratory, University of Cambridge; 82*b* Trevor Hill; 82*r* ZEFA/ Freytag; 84*t*, 84*b* Trevor Hill; 84/85 Graham Portlock; 86*l*, 86*r* MEPL; 87*t* Science Photo Library/ Dr. Jeremy Burgess; 87*b* MEPL; 88*t* Scala/ Museo della Scienza/ Firenze; 89*t* Science Photo Library/ NASA; 89*b* Ann Ronan Picture Library 92, 93, 94, 95 NHM Picture Library; 96 MEPL; 98, 99 ZEFA/ U.W.S.;104 Roy L Bishop, Arcadia University; 108 Science Photo Library/ Philippe Plailly; 109 Science Photo Library/ Paul Shambroom; 110, 112, 113 Graham Portlock; 117 Science Photo Library/ Peter Menzel; 119 Ann Ronan/ Image Select; 122 Michael Holford; 123 Science Photo Library/ Adam Hart-Davis; 124, 125 MEPL; 128*l* Graham Portlock; 128*r* Science Photo Library/ US Dept of Energy; 132 ZEFA/ Bramaz; 133 top Science Photo Library; 133*tl*, 133*tr*, 133*bl* ZEFA; 133*cl*, 133*br* Bruce Coleman/ Kim Taylor, Jules Cowan; 134, 135 Trevor Hill; 140*t* Holt Studios/ Nigel Cattlin; 140*b* NHPA/ Anthony Bannister; 141*t* NHPA/ Stephen Dalton, Ron Fotheringham; 141*bl* Trevor Hill; 141*br* Science Photo Library/ Alfred Pasieka; 142 NHPA/ E.A. James;143*t* OSF/ Godfrey Merlen; 143*b* NHPA/ E.A. James; 144, 145*l* MEPL; 145*r* Science Photo Library/ Chris Priest & Mark Clarke; 146, 147 Science Photo Library; 150 Science Photo Library/ CNRI; 152*l* MEPL; 152*r* Trevor Hill; 153*t* MEPL; 153*b* Athlone Laboratories; 153 NHPA/ Peter Parks; 155 Science Photo Library/ CNRI

Designed by Pardoe Blacker Publishing Ltd,
Shawlands Court, Newchapel Road, Lingfield, Surrey RH7 6BL
Illustrated by Gary Andrews, Arcana Studios, Annabelle Brend,
Dawn Brend, Neil Bulpitt, Harry Clow, Charlotte Cruise, Jeff Edwards,
Jon Eland, Chris Forsey, Geoff Jones, Deborah Maizels, Roddy Murray,
Nick Raven, Martin Sanders
Indexed by Indexing Specialists, 202 Church Road,
Hove, East Sussex BN3 2DJ

C o n t e n t s

Contents

Measurement

Scientists depend on making measurements. What is the temperature of this liquid? What is its volume? What is its mass?

Standard units of measurement

Imagine that you have a length of string. You have to tell someone how long it is without showing it to them or using a ruler. You could say 'It is four times longer than my first finger' or you could say 'It is the same length as the side of the school atlas'.

Which of the two would be the most accurate method of measuring the length? Would either of these methods be suitable for general measurements? What if your finger grows? How would someone in Australia know how long your finger was? Imagine the announcement in *Concorde*: 'We are now cruising at a height of 38 000 school atlases at a speed of 14 000 000 Rajwinder Sarkar forefingers per hour.'

This is obviously silly. If you are going to measure something you need to have a standard unit of measurement that everyone understands and that does not vary.

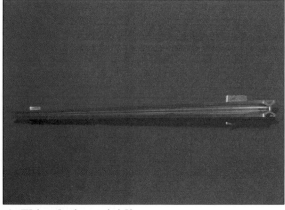

North pole
Paris
Equator

◀ *A metre was once defined as one ten-millionth of the distance from the North pole to the equator.*

Length and the metre

You will be familiar with a metre rule, but just what is a metre? In 1791, French scientists proposed the metre as the basis of measurement of length. They defined it as one ten-millionth of the distance from the North Pole to the Equator through Paris. This distance was rather difficult to measure – no-one actually reached the North Pole until 1909! But in 1792 two scientists, Jean-Baptiste Delambre and Pierre Mechain, set about estimating it, by making an accurate measurement of the distance from Dunkirk to Barcelona. Later, however, the metre was defined as the distance between two lines engraved on a specially made platinum-iridium bar.

▲ *This platinum-iridium bar was used to define a length of 1m.*

By 1960 a more accurate standard had been developed. The metre was redefined as the length of 1 650 763.73 wavelengths of the orange-red light produced by atoms of krypton (a rare gas). But by 1983 the metre had been redefined again, this time as the distance travelled by light in one 299 972 458th part of a second.

▶ *The standard kilogram is a cylinder made from 90% platinum and 10% iridium. It is 39mm tall and has a diameter of 39mm.*

Mass and the kilogram

The standard unit of mass used by all scientists is kept at the International Bureau of Weights and Measures at Sèvres, near Paris, France. It is a special block of platinum–iridium alloy, which is agreed to have a mass of one kilogram. Copies of this mass have been sent to laboratories all over the world, so that the masses of other objects can be compared with it.

Time and the second

Measurements of time are needed to answer two main questions: 'When did it happen?' and 'How long did it last?' For centuries the rotation of the Earth has been used for measuring time. The period of time during which the Earth makes one complete rotation on its axis is known as a day.

▶ *This graph shows that clocks have got more accurate over the years. The first pendulum clock lost 1 second in 3 hours.*

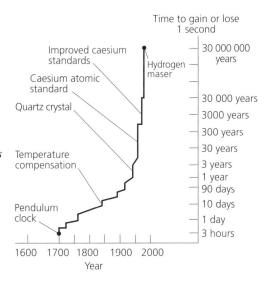

Clocks and watches are made to copy this rotation of the Earth. For example, the time taken by two revolutions of the hour hand of a watch is equal to the time for one revolution of the Earth. (Why do you think *two* revolutions are used, rather than one?) The early rotating clocks and watches do not give a very accurate standard of time. Now atomic clocks are used as standards. The SI unit of time is a second. In 1967 the standard for the second was set as the time occupied by 9 192 631 770 vibrations of the light produced by a type of atom called caesium-133.

Unit name	Physical quantity
metre (m)	length
kilogram (kg)	mass
seconds (s)	time
ampere (A)	electric current
kelvin (K)	themodynamic temperature
candela (cd)	luminous intensity
mole (mol)	amount of substance

▲ *These are the SI units. They are used worldwide for scientific measurements.*

SI Units

SI units are the standard units of measurement used all over the world. They were adopted by an international conference in 1960 to end the confusion caused by different people using different units. There are seven base SI units. As you have seen, the units were first defined in terms of a particular example like the standard metre bar, kept in Paris. As greater standards of accuracy were required the units were redefined as measurements of physical phenomena.

Prefix	Symbol	Meaning
mega	M	one million times the quantity
kilo	k	one thousand times the quantity
centi	c	one-hundredth of the quantity
milli	m	one-thousandth of the quantity

Examples:

1/100 of a metre = 1 centimetre

1 kilogram (1 kg) = 1000 grams

▲ *Some measurement prefixes and their meanings.*

HOW HOT is it?

It is often important to know the hotness of a substance. Finding out the hotness of a substance is something we do every day.

▲ *Some people estimate how hot things are, like testing bath water with their elbow.*

Thermometers and scales

These methods are not accurate ways of finding the hotness of a substance, but they do give a rough idea. The 'hotness' of something is called its **temperature**, and to measure the temperature accurately an instrument called a **thermometer** is used. Many thermometers give a reading of the temperature in degrees Celsius, which is written °C.

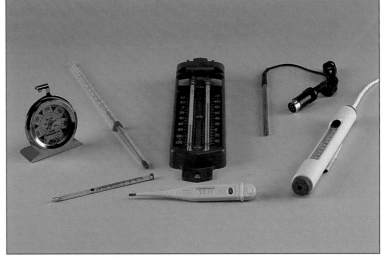

▲ *Different types of thermometer; in the foreground is a digital clinical thermometer. Going clockwise from this are a mercury-in-glass thermometer, a bimetallic strip oven thermometer, an alcohol-in-glass thermometer, a maximum-minimum weather thermometer, a probe which plugs into a computer and an alcohol-in-glass floating pool thermometer.*

All thermometers make use of some property of a substance that changes as the temperature changes. These properties are called **thermometric properties**.

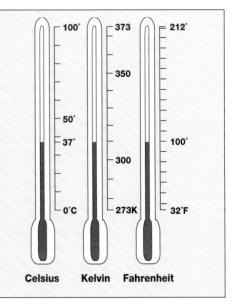

▶ *A comparison of the temperature scales. 0°C is equivalent to 273K and 32°F.*

Celsius   Kelvin   Fahrenheit

TEMPERATURE SCALES

The Celsius temperature scale used to be called the Centigrade scale but its name was changed in 1948. It is named after the Swedish astronomer Anders Celsius (1701–44). Anders Celsius had proposed a Centigrade scale that specified water freezing at 100 and water boiling at 0. These were switched by J. P. Christin in 1743 to give the scale we know today. Other temperature scales include the thermodynamic scale which gives the temperature in kelvins, written K, and the Fahrenheit scale which gives the temperature in degrees Fahrenheit, written °F.

*T*he Kelvin temperature scale is named after Lord Kelvin. He was called William Thomson, until he was knighted in 1867. He became professor of natural philosophy at the University of Glasgow when he was only 22, and held the post for 53 years. He invented many important measuring instruments, including some of the first accurate meters for electrical measurements. In 1851 he proposed the idea of absolute zero – the lowest possible temperature. This temperature is now the zero of the Kelvin scale (= −273 °C). He also worked with many leading scientists of the day, including James Joule (who the unit of energy is named after.) Kelvin created the first laboratory to be used for teaching science in Britain where he was a formidable teacher. He used a small box with three compartments. He would put cards bearing the names of all the students in the compartment marked 'not called'. Then he would take a card at random and ask the student named on it a question about a previous lecture. If the answer was satisfactory the card was put into the compartment marked 'passed'. If it wasn't the card went into the box marked 'called not passed'. The question was then passed around the class until someone answered it satisfactorily. The three boxes were known by the students as Purgatory, Heaven and Hell.

Thermometric properties

One property that is commonly used is the expansion of liquids as they get hotter. As the liquid in the thermometer gets hotter it expands and moves further up the tube.

The temperatures of melting ice and steam are called **fixed points**. On the Celsius scale, at atmospheric pressure, the temperature at which ice melts is called 0 °C, and the temperature at which water boils is called 100 °C.

▼ *Calibrating the lower fixed point (0 °C) and the upper fixed point (100 °C).*

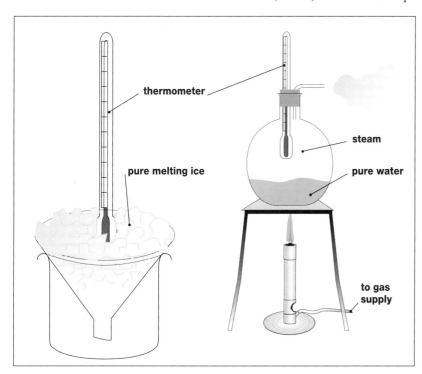

thermometer

pure melting ice

steam

pure water

to gas supply

What is the difference between heat and temperature?

Heat is a transfer of energy. When you put a beaker of water on a Bunsen burner, the flame of the Bunsen transfers energy to the water. This transfer of energy is called **heat**. The effect of the heat is to raise the temperature of the water perhaps enough to change its state from liquid to gas. You need to supply 4200 joules (J) of heat to change the temperature of 1 kg of water by 1 °C. This gives a pointer to the difference between heat and temperature; they are quite different things measured in different units: Heat is measured in joules; temperature is measured in degrees Celsius.

One easy way to demonstrate the difference between the heat and temperature is to set up two identical Bunsen burners with identical flames and put identical 1-litre beakers over each Bunsen for the same length of time. If one beaker holds 100 g of water and the other beaker holds 1000 g of water you will notice a significant difference in their temperatures after a few minutes, even though they have both been supplied with the same amount of heat.

KEEPING

Why do things get dirty?

Advertisements constantly tell us how to clean things – skin, hair, teeth, working surfaces, dishes and clothes are just a few examples. But why do they get dirty?

Of course, things like paint, food, ink and milk get spilt, and have to be wiped up. But most cleaning in our homes concentrates on removing grease. People's skin produces a greasy material called **sebum**, which keeps it supple and waterproof. Sebum gets on clothing and fabrics, furniture and paintwork . . . greasy fingermarks get everywhere! Much of our food contains oils and fats, and these make dishes, kitchen surfaces and even our teeth greasy. The atmosphere contains a lot of dust particles, and these stick to greasy and damp surfaces. So, the cleaning materials we use have to be able to remove grease as well as particles of dirt.

▼ *Wet soap is dried and cut into noodles. These are then mixed with perfumes, colours, oils and creams to a detailed formula.*

Soaps

Soap was one of the earliest recorded cleaning agents, first used about 4500 years ago. The wrapped bar of soap came into use only at the beginning of the 20th century.

Soaps are made by boiling plant oils, such as palm oil, olive oil or castor oil, or animal fats with a strong **alkali** such as sodium hydroxide or potassium hydroxide. When this mixture cools, the soap solidifies on the surface and can be skimmed off, washed and dried, coloured and perfumed and moulded into bars.

Oven cleaners contain a strong alkali, such as sodium hydroxide. This combines with the fat on the surface of the oven to form a soap. This is soluble in water, so it can be washed away. The fat is **emulsified**.

Toothpastes contain soap. The weakly alkaline nature of these **neutralises** the acids which are produced by bacteria present in the mouth.

Clean

Detergents

There is another important group of cleaning materials, called **detergents**. These can dissolve in both water and grease, and so make grease mix with water. This is called **emulsification**. Detergents are said to be able to emulsify grease and dirt.

Cleaning clothes can be hard work. In less developed parts of the world, people have to go to the river bank, hold their dirty clothes under water and rub and beat them with stones to break up and remove the grease and dirt. But for most of us detergents have made cleaning much easier. (The name 'detergent' comes from a Latin word meaning 'to wipe off'.) Detergents are made quite differently from soaps, starting with **hydrocarbons** – substances containing only hydrogen and carbon. They are obtained from crude oil, and are made to react with sulphuric acid.

ADVANTAGES OF DETERGENTS

Detergents have some advantages over soaps. For example, they work better than soap in 'hard' water. Hard water contains calcium and magnesium, which come from dissolved rocks. Soap combines with the calcium or magnesium to produce an **insoluble** solid called scum – this makes it difficult to form a lather.

If you want to clean things with soap in hard water, you need to 'soften' the water first. This can be done by adding sodium carbonate to the water. The sodium carbonate combines with the calcium and magnesium and prevents them from reacting with the soap to form scum. Otherwise you have to go on adding soap until all the calcium and magnesium has reacted; only after that can the lather form, and the soap start working as an emulsifier. Detergents don't react with calcium or magnesium, so they don't make scum.

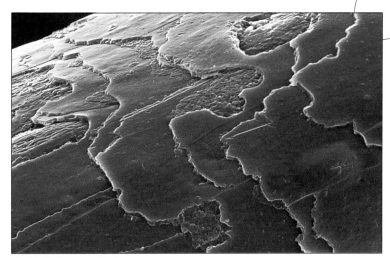

▲ *This human hair is magnified 600× and shows the outer scales. These are thought to stop hairs from matting together.*

WE USE DETERGENTS EVERY DAY

Cleaning hair and fabrics with soap can produce real problems. Hair has an outer scaly surface, like fish scales. The edges of the scales point towards the tip of the hair, and these scales open and close depending on what sort of liquid is in contact with the hair. In weakly alkaline solutions the hair scales open up.

If you wash your hair with soap (don't try it!) it will look rough, and you will find it difficult to comb or brush. This is because soap solution is slightly alkaline, and in hard water the opened-up scales get entangled with the scum.

Shampoos are detergents which are either neutral or weakly acidic. These don't form a scum with water, and their acidity makes the hair scales close up. So your hair feels soft and smooth, and is easier to comb. For similar reasons soapless detergents are better than soaps for fabrics.

There are many other cleaning materials used in and around the home. Maybe when you've washed your hair, had a bath, cleaned your teeth, done the dishes and wiped down the kitchen work surfaces you'll find time to investigate them further!

■ *For more about acids see p84–85.*

eating

All animals feed – and that includes you! Animals get everything they need for growth, repair and development from the **nutrients** in their food. The major groups of nutrients are **proteins**, **carbohydrates**, **fats**, **minerals** and **vitamins**. We also need to drink enough water and to eat enough fibre to keep the bowel healthy. Everyone should try to understand something about the nutrients they should get in their food. If you don't have these nutrients, or if you have them in the wrong amounts, you won't stay healthy for long.

An obvious requirement for a healthy life is that you have enough to eat. Sadly, many people don't. Television pictures from famine-stricken countries show people dying from **starvation**. Famines usually follow disasters, like a war or a crop failure, due to lack of rain. Millions of people *never* get enough of the nutrients they need, and are therefore ill or in pain all the time. They are suffering from **malnutrition** (bad nutrition).

Malnutrition is widespread

Tragically, malnutrition is widespread. This map of the world shows places where most people get enough protein in their diet and places where many people don't. Proteins are vital. They provide the raw materials your body needs to build new cells and repair damaged cells. People in Africa, Asia and South America often depend on the food they grow for themselves, so droughts affect them directly and immediately. People who don't eat enough protein may get diseases more easily because their natural body defences don't work well. Children who don't eat enough protein

don't grow properly.

Fresh foods like fish, fruit and vegetables are important for keeping us healthy because they are rich in minerals and vitamins. It is interesting to see that people eating one of the healthiest diets in Europe live in one of the poorest areas: southern Italy. They eat plenty of vegetables, seafood, pasta, tomatoes and citrus fruits like oranges and lemons which are rich in vitamin C.

Key

Areas where food is plentiful

Areas where malnutrition is common

in rainforest areas, the main foods are derived from rice, vegetable oils, citrus fruits, bananas, coffee, tea and cocoa

in desert areas the main foods are derived from sheep, goats, and wheat

well

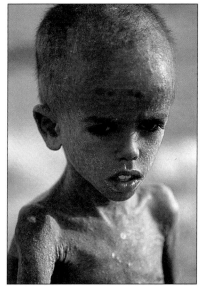

▲ *Starvation is not the same as malnutrition. Starvation means not getting enough food to keep you alive.*

A *healthy diet in the Developing World*

Many poorer people in the Developing World eat a very healthy diet in a good year when food is plentiful. This is because they may eat lots of home-grown fruit and vegetables and lots of peas and beans – either fresh or dried – which are rich in proteins. In Africa the meat may be wild gazelle or goat rather than beef or chicken.

in Savanna areas the main foods are derived from cattle, pigs, poultry, maize, vegetable oils and sugar cane.

■ *For more about diet see pp14–15*

EATING *to*

You can see from the graph on the right that heart disease has become more common in Britain since 1950. The graph below shows the death rates from heart disease in different parts of the world. Clearly, North America and Europe have much higher rates of heart disease than South America and Asia. Why?

The answer may lie in the amount and type of food that is eaten. Most people in North America and Britain get enough to eat, but in some ways they eat too much. A clue to this puzzle may be found in the table (on the right) showing the food intake in calories for people in different countries. There seems to be a general pattern that the countries where the food intake is highest have high death rates from heart disease.

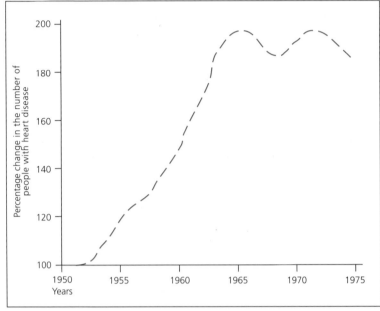

▲ *The death rate from heart disease has increased since 1950.*

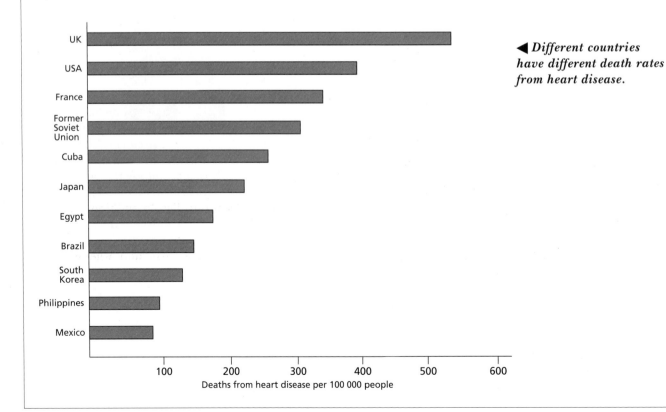

◀ *Different countries have different death rates from heart disease.*

Deaths from heart disease per 100 000 people

your HEART'S *content!*

DID YOU KNOW?

In 1982 the World Health Organisation recommended that people in Britain should cut the amount of saturated fat they eat by half. Saturated fats are contained in animal fats such as butter and lard.

Risk factor	Effect on body	End result
eating and drinking alcohol too much, not exercising enough	overweight	**high risk of heart disease**
high fat content of food	high fat level in blood	
high salt content of food	high blood pressure	
smoking	speeds up damage to arteries	
stress	high blood pressure	

▲ *Scientists are trying to discover what causes heart disease and why it is so common in Britain yet rare in Africa or Asia. They now think that there are several factors that can lead to heart disease.*

Country	Average daily food intake per person (calories)
USA	3500 – 4000
UK	3000 – 3500
France	3000 – 3500
Former Soviet Union	3000 – 3500
Cuba	3000 – 3500
Japan	2500 – 3000
Egypt	2500 – 3000
Brazil	2500 – 3000
South Korea	2500 – 3000
Mexico	2500 – 3000
Philippines	2000 – 2500

Cause and effect

It's also worth noting that people in Africa and Asia don't eat nearly as much fat and sugar as we do in Britain. In wealthier countries, people tend to eat more foods like sweets, chocolate, cakes, crisps and snacks – all foods that are high in fat or sugar, or often both. Remember, eating only poor-quality food (sometimes called 'junk food') won't help your body to grow properly or stay healthy. The information here doesn't prove that eating too much, particularly of fats and sugars, causes heart disease. However, it does make us look carefully at our diet. In addition, scientists are looking at the effect on the heart of our general lifestyle including the amount of exercise people take, and whether they smoke or drink alcohol.

■ *For more about the heart see pp20–21.*

What are you like INSIDE?

Science has enabled us to measure various things about the body. For example, using a thermometer can tell us if the body temperature is normal or not.

Knowing the blood pressure and body temperature, and knowing how the heart is beating, can help a doctor assess the general health of the person.

Other techniques have been developed which allow us to see inside the body.

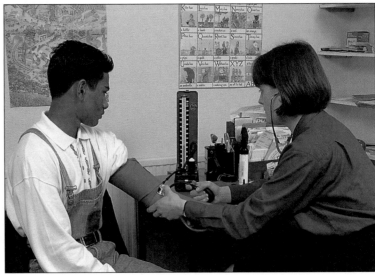

▲ *We can measure blood pressure using a sphygmomanometer or listen to someone's heart by using a stethoscope.*

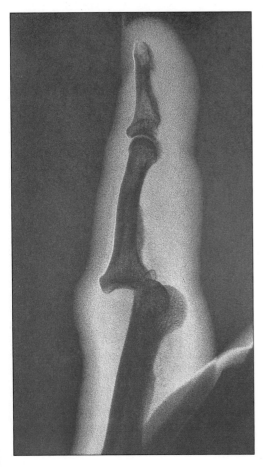

◄ *This coloured X-ray shows a dislocated finger.*

X-rays

X-rays were discovered in 1895 by Wilhelm Röntgen. The first X-ray pictures of the human body were taken a few months later, and this technique has been used ever since. X-rays pass through human flesh, but bones show up clearly because they are more dense and the rays cannot pass through them.

X-ray photographs can be improved by computers, so that it is possible to see the soft tissues clearly as well as the bones. A special way of using X-rays is the technique called **computed tomography** (CT). This gives a picture of a complete cross-section of the patient's body.

■ *For more about X-rays see p105.*

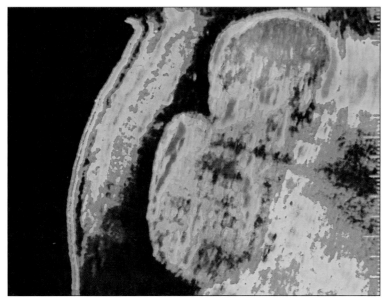

Ultrasound

Ultrasound is sound at a high frequency, too high for us to hear. A special device produces this sound as it rests on the skin. The sound penetrates the body. Some of the sound is reflected back and can be turned into a picture. We can even use ultrasound to get a moving picture of what is inside the body. The technique is used to see babies developing in the womb. We can actually see a baby's heart beating, or movements of its tiny fingers and toes!

■ *For more about ultrasound see p61.*

▲ *A false-colour ultrasound image showing the back view of a 21-week-old foetus.*

Light in medicine

An **endoscope** is used by doctors to look inside the body. This device uses **optical fibres** which carry light around corners or bends. So if one end of the device is swallowed by a patient, light can pass down the fibre and shine on to the surface of the stomach – it is like having a long, thin torch. A doctor can look at the image at the receiving end of the endoscope to see if there is an ulcer in the stomach lining, for example.

■ *For more about optical fibres see pp106–7.*

▶ *Here the blue glow of a laser is used to remove fatty deposits from the coronary artery. Slightly above the laser is a hollow tube through which oxygen may be fed and toxic substances removed.*

Lasers

Lasers are devices that produce a type of light that is so intense that it can be used to destroy diseased cells. Laser light can also be sent down an endoscope, so if diseased cells can be seen with an endoscope they can be destroyed using a laser.

A laser can also be used to unblock an artery which has a blood clot in it. Blockages like these can cause heart attacks. An optical fibre is threaded along the artery and when a blockage is found a tiny burst of laser light is fired to try to remove the blockage.

■ *For more about laser light see pp108–9.*

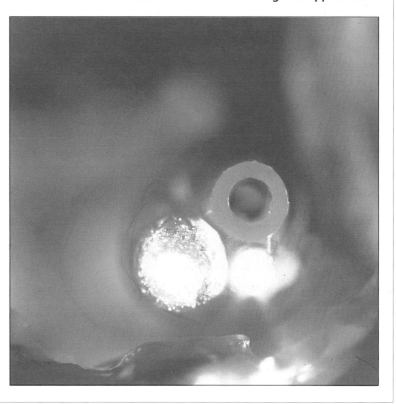

Movement, mus

Support

All living organisms are able to move and support their structures. Plants rely on water in their cells and thick cell walls to hold them up. Some animals rely on the buoyancy effects of water to support them, for example jellyfish and large molluscs (members of the same group as the snails and slugs) like the octopus live in water quite happily, but their bodies lack support out of water. Animals which live on land need to support their own bodies. Animal bodies are supported using a skeleton.

There are two types of skeleton, the **external skeleton** (found in insects) and the **internal skeleton** (found in mammals, birds, reptiles, amphibians and bony fish). The internal skeleton is made from bones. The big advantage of the internal skeleton is that the bone is living material, it grows as the animal grows. The insect has to shed its skeleton as it grows and produce a new skeleton each time, just like getting a new suit of armour!

▲ *Jellyfish cannot support their own weight out of water.*

▶ *Ball and socket joints allow a circular movement; hinge joints allow less movement like a door on a hinge.*

ball and socket joint

hinge joint

ball and socket joint

muscle

Skeleton

The skeleton of a mammal has a number of jobs to do:
● The bones support (hold up) the soft parts of the body;
● Some bones protect delicate organs like the brain or heart;
● The way the bones are connected allows the body to move efficiently.

Individual bones are firm strong structures. The point where two bones connect is called a **joint**. The position of the joints allows movement. The human hand, for example, can be rotated 180° by a combination of movement of the wrist joints, the elbow joint and the shoulder joint.

cles and joints

Muscles

The bones can move only because of the presence of **muscles**. Muscle is a special animal **tissue**. It has the ability to contract (get shorter). Certain types of muscles are always attached to bones. These are called **skeletal muscles**. The muscles are often connected in pairs. This is because a muscle can only pull, it does this by getting shorter. The muscle can't push, so to return a bone to its original position another muscle must pull the bone back.

Antagonistic muscles

The two muscles appear to work against one another. When one muscle **contracts**, the other must be **relaxed** (not contracting). Then to return the bone to its original position, the first muscle must relax and the other muscle must contract. Whatever one muscle is doing, the other is doing the opposite. For this reason these pairs of muscles are often called **antagonistic pairs** (antagonistic means 'working against each other').

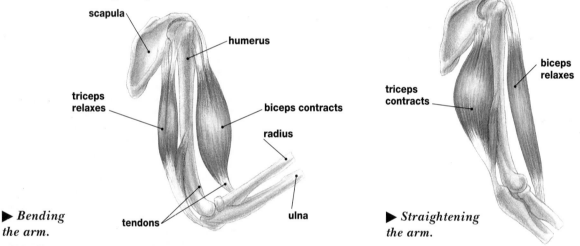

scapula

humerus

triceps relaxes

biceps contracts

radius

tendons

ulna

▶ *Bending the arm.*

triceps contracts

biceps relaxes

▶ *Straightening the arm.*

Synovial joints

Nearly all the joints in the body are in constant use. The stresses and strains on the major joints of the body are enormous. Two sets of bones moving against one another would quickly wear out without some sort of lubrication.

All the big joints in the limbs are **synovial joints**. These are joints which are wrapped in a tough layer of **membranes** containing **ligaments**. The ligaments hold the bones together and form a seal around the joint. The end of each bone is covered with **cartilage**; this tough but elastic tissue prevents the solid bones from rubbing against each other. Inside the joint is also a special membrane called the **synovial membrane** which secretes a fluid. This fluid lubricates the joint and acts as a shock absorber. Without these special joints many sports would probably be impossible to play!

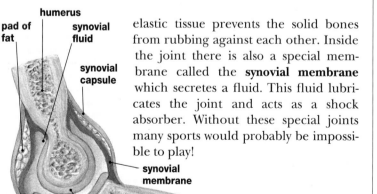

humerus

pad of fat

synovial fluid

synovial capsule

synovial membrane

cartilage   ulna

◀ *Ball and socket and hinge joints are examples of synovial joints.*

Heart and

The heart and blood circulation

One of William Harvey's most important ideas was that blood flows round the body continuously pumped by the heart. He worked it out by measuring the amount of blood which could be contained in the heart. Then he estimated how much blood is pushed out of the heart at each beat. He knew the number of beats the heart made in one hour. So he was able to work out that, in theory, the amount of blood sent out from the heart every half-hour was greater then the total volume that could be contained in the whole body. Since this was ridiculous, he decided the blood must go round and round.

Arteries and veins

Harvey also knew that the big blood vessels, the **arteries** and the **veins**, connected together. From his knowledge and from the experiments he performed he worked out the direction in which the blood flowed, and the reason why **valves** are present in the veins and the heart. He had found valves in the dissections he had done and had demonstrated how they work. In his book, Harvey made all the key points

William Harvey was an English physician born in 1578. He worked out how the human circulatory system functions by observing and dissecting the hearts of many different animals and by using his observations to study his patients. In some cases he was also able to study them after they had died.

about the circulation clear: the **ventricles** pump blood to the arteries, blood travels from veins into arteries via the heart, and blood circulates from the heart to the lungs, and back to the heart.

Blood capillaries

There was only one thing about the circulation that Harvey failed to explain; how blood passed from arteries into veins in the organs of the body. He knew it had to happen, but the discovery of the connections had to wait until microscopes were invented which were powerful enough to see the blood **capillaries**. This happened in 1661, four years after Harvey's death.

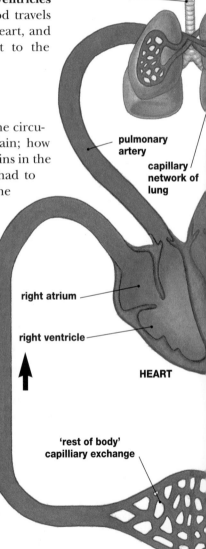

trachea

pulmonary artery

capillary network of lung

right atrium

right ventricle

HEART

■ deoxygenated blood

■ oxygenated blood

vena cava

'rest of body' capilliary exchange

to the heart

◀ *Blood flowing upwards pushes the valve open. Blood trying to flow downwards pushes the valve shut.*

Circulation

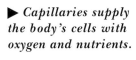

▶ *Capillaries supply the body's cells with oxygen and nutrients.*

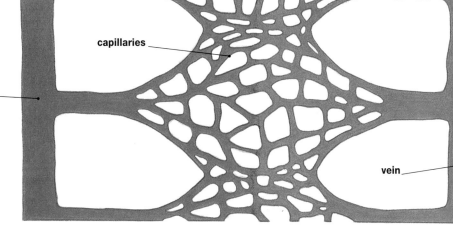

capillaries

artery

vein

pulmonary vein

left lung

left atrium

left ventricle

aorta

What are capillaries?

These are the tiny blood vessels which link the arteries with the veins. When a large artery enters an organ of the body, such as the liver or brain, the artery divides into two, then into four, then eight, and so on, to give microscopically small, thin blood vessels. These tiny capillaries reach between individual cells and supply the cells with dissolved oxygen and nutrients like sugars.

Heart transplants

Doctors have developed the technique of transplanting whole hearts from one person to another. This is done usually when a person has very bad heart disease which

◀ *One side of our heart pumps blood towards the lungs, the other side pumps blood around the rest of the organs of the body. If we take any point in the body's circulatory system and trace a path around the system until we arrive back at the same point, (remembering that the circulatory system is a one-way system), we would travel through the heart twice. This is known as a* **double circulation.**

cannot be treated in any other way. A donor heart has to be found – this is often taken from road accident victims or people who may have died suddenly from known causes. Obviously the heart from the donor person must be unaffected by either the accident or other cause of death. The person who is having the transplant is first connected to a heart/lung machine. This machine keeps the blood flowing around the body and keeps the lungs ventilated while the donor's heart is removed. Then artery by artery and vein by vein the new heart is sewn into place.

ACCEPTING THE HEART

Once the new heart is in place the biggest problem is whether the rest of the body accepts it. The body's defences will attack anything which is not recognised as belonging to or part of the body. So transplanted organs are recognised as foreign and will be attacked. For this reason, the patient has to have specific drugs which prevent the body's defences attacking the new heart. This is the time when the patient has to be careful not to catch colds or other infections. As time passes the risks gradually get fewer. Many heart transplant patients recover to lead full, active lives.

■ *For more about heart disease see pp14–15.*

EXCRETION:

*When a cell uses the nutrients that it needs it produces waste products. This happens when a cell uses **glucose** sugar to transfer energy in a process called **respiration**. Glucose combines with oxygen and produces carbon dioxide, water and transfers energy.*

Removing carbon dioxide

The water and the energy produced when glucose combines with oxygen are useful to the cell, but the carbon dioxide must be removed. In humans the carbon dioxide leaves each cell and enters the bloodstream. The blood carries the carbon dioxide to the lungs where the carbon dioxide leaves the bloodstream and is breathed out into the air. This is an example of **excretion**. Excretion means the removal from the body of substances which the cells have produced which might be harmful. So the lungs are organs of excretion as well as organs of **gaseous exchange**.

Removing urea

There are other substances produced by cells which must be removed from the body, for example a substance called **urea**. Urea is made in the liver from carbon dioxide and **ammonia**. Ammonia is a very poisonous substance and must be removed quickly. First, the ammonia is turned into urea because urea can be transported in the bloodstream whereas ammonia damages the body. The blood carrying the urea eventually finds its way into the body's two kidneys. Kidneys, in humans, are two organs at the back of the abdomen, on either side of the spine.

The kidney is an amazing organ. It filters out the urea from the bloodstream and controls the amount of water in your body.

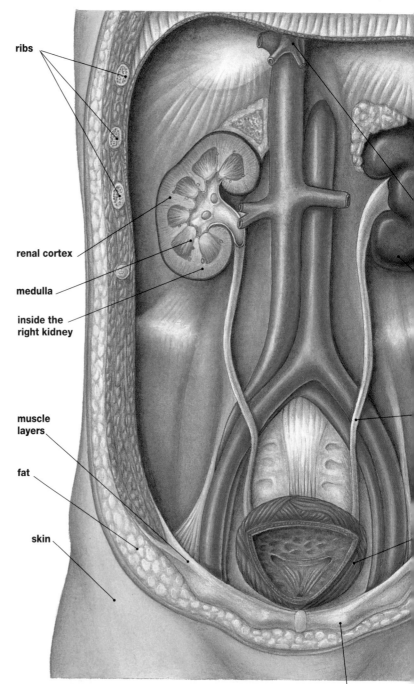

ribs

renal cortex

medulla

inside the
right kidney

muscle
layers

fat

skin

pelvis

▲ *The kidney produces a solution of urea in water called **urine**. This fluid leaves the kidney and is held in the bladder until we go to the lavatory. The kidney does a vital job.*

Waste *from* CELLS

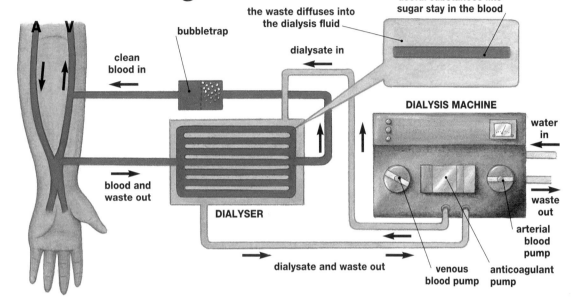

the waste diffuses into the dialysis fluid

useful substances like sugar stay in the blood

bubbletrap

clean blood in

dialysate in

A V

blood and waste out

DIALYSER

DIALYSIS MACHINE

water in

waste out

arterial blood pump

dialysate and waste out

venous blood pump

anticoagulant pump

diaphragm

vena cava

left kidney

ureter

bladder

▲ *The dialysis machine filters the blood by removing waste, but allows useful substances to stay in the blood.*

Dialysis

People unfortunate enough to suffer kidney failure require treatment to filter their blood using a procedure called **dialysis**. Each treatment can take 5 or 6 hours twice a week during which time blood is removed from their body and circulated through a filtering unit, then returned to the body.

Kidney transplants

Many people who suffer from this condition would prefer to have a kidney transplant. This is an operation where a healthy kidney, either from a relative (we all have two kidneys and can survive quite happily with one) or the victim of an accident, can

be donated and transplanted into the body of the patient. Once the blood vessels are connected up, and provided the kidney isn't rejected (the body's defences sometimes attack transplanted organs), the new kidney will work in place of the damaged kidneys.

The kidney is a vital organ. Without it the poison produced by the activities of the body's cells would accumulate and kill cells in the body.

Egestion is not excretion

One point to remember about excretion is that the one bodily function which most people think of when they think of excretion is not excretion at all! The removal of solid waste, **faeces**, from the end of the digestive system is not excretion but **egestion**. This is because the undigested food has not actually been inside a living cell, it has not been processed at all by a cell, it has simply passed all the way through the digestive system.

◀ *Some people carry a card which says that if they should be killed in an accident they are willing for their organs to be used for transplantation.*

CELLS AND SPECIALISATION

Our bodies contain around a thousand million million cells. Cells could not be seen until microscopes were invented in the 17th century as they are only around one-hundredth of a millimetre across. Cells are the smallest living units able to carry out all the basic functions of life, mainly growth, metabolism and reproduction. Cells are specialised to carry out certain jobs in both animals and plants.

Animal cells

Animal cells are not tough and do not have regular shapes. They all contain a cell membrane and a **nucleus** (except some red blood cells). There are a tremendous number of different types of animal cells, each type with a different job to do.

NERVE CELLS

The **nerve cell** is a very special type of cell. The shape of the nerve cell gives us a clue to what it does: it has a very irregular shape with lots of strands reaching out towards other cells. The nerve cell carries information in the form of tiny bursts of electrical current. This information is passed on to neighbouring cells through these long strands. All the normal parts of an animal cell are present.

nucleus

cytoplasm

layer of jelly

diameter = 0.1 mm

vacuole containing enzymes

length = 0.05 mm

▲ *The ovum (top) and the sperm cell (right). An ovum is about the size of a full stop.*

tail

GAMETES

Two other animal cells which are specially adapted to do their jobs are the cells involved in **fertilisation**. The sex cells, or **gametes**, produced by human beings are called **spermatozoa** or sperm cells (in males) and **ova** or 'egg' cells (in females). There are big differences in the size and shape of these two types of cell, but each contains the basic parts that all animal cells contain.

Sperm cells are highly **motile** (they can swim) whereas the ova cells are not motile and are moved through the **oviduct** by the movements of other cells. For animal cells, the ova cells are very large. The reasons for this are linked with the events which follow successful fertilisation (when a single sperm cell merges with a single ovum cell). When fertilisation takes place, the egg cell must divide and continue dividing to produce a large ball of cells. Stored nutrients in the egg cell provide the energy for

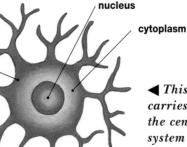

insulating layer made by another cell wrapped around the axon

dendrites - these contact other nerve cells around them

nucleus

cell membrane

cytoplasm

nerve ending

axon - this carries the electrical messages

◄ *This nerve cell carries messages from the central nervous system to a muscle.*

these divisions. Therefore, it is essential that the egg cell contains a good store of energy-supplying nutrients; this in turn means that the cell **cytoplasm** must be large.

CHROMOSOMES

One other way in which these cells are specially adapted to do their job cannot be seen easily. The nucleus of each sex cell contains half the number of **chromosomes** present in all other cells of the body. This is important because when a sperm cell and ovum cell merge together the number of chromosomes must add together to give the total that is in all cells.

▶ *Chromosomes are made from DNA. They are the 'plans' from which cells work.*

nucleus

cell

chromosomes

▲ *The nucleus contains chromosomes.*

enlarged chromosome

CILIATED CELLS

One other highly specialised cell is the **ciliated epithelial cell**. This cell is a lining cell found on the surface of an organ (this is what epithelial means). It has tiny 'hairs' which stick out from the cell and these 'hairs' wave in a precise rhythm.

When large numbers of these cells are found side by side they can create a current of fluid or air. These are the cells which cause the ovum to move along the oviduct towards the **uterus**. Here, if the ovum has been fertilised, it may stick to the wall and begin to develop.

In the windpipe there are also millions of ciliated epithelial cells. Their continuous movements waft the **mucus** (a thick fluid lining the air passage) upwards to the back of the throat. This mucus helps to trap dust and bacterial cells. Smoking damages these cells and over a period of time they become less effective and many may also die.

In our bodies cells are specialised and organised into the different systems that we have been looking at like the cardiovascular, muscle and kidney systems (*see* pp18–23).

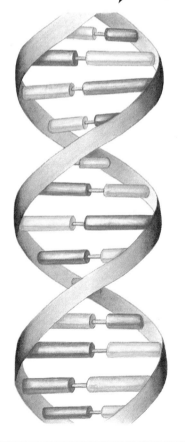

◀ *DNA is a store of genetic information. It contains the instructions to pass on characteristics from one generation to the next and to make the molecules needed for growth and development.*

▶ *A false-colour image of a section of the windpipe (trachea). The ciliated cells, coloured green, move mucus upwards to the back of the throat keeping the lungs and airways free.*

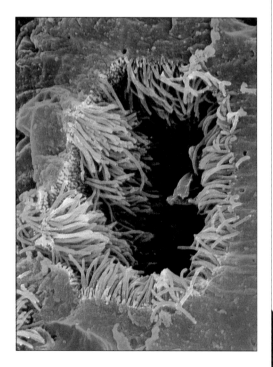

CELLS AND SPECIALISATION

ℙ*lant cells*

Plant cells are different from animal cells in a major way: plant cells have a cell wall. This is a tough layer made from a substance called **cellulose**. The wall gives a plant cell its shape and its toughness. Inside the plant cell there is also a nucleus, cytoplasm, a membrane (a very thin layer inside the cell wall) and in some plant cells (green ones) small oval structures which are green in colour called **chloroplasts**.

Plant cells are specialised so that they are able to do particular jobs.

LEAF STRUCTURE

The leaf of a plant is adapted to absorb light very efficiently. Leaves contain cells in layers (*see* diagram below). The cells in the top layer are called **palisade** cells. They contain lots of chloroplasts. This is important because it is the green colour in the

▶ *This section through a leaf shows the palisade mesophyll layer (see below).*

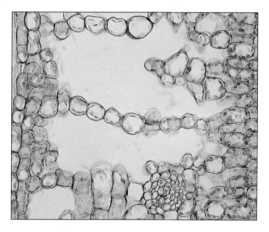

chloroplasts that absorbs the sunlight which provides the energy for photosynthesis. The palisade cells are very close together, making sure that the maximum amount of light is absorbed as it strikes the leaf surface.

On the lower surface there are special holes called **stomatal pores**. These pores allow gases, like carbon dioxide, to enter the leaf. The air spaces in the leaf allow the carbon dioxide to **diffuse** (spread around) the whole of the leaf and reach all the cells.

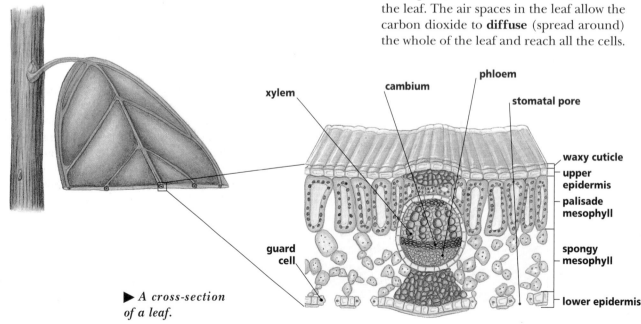

xylem   cambium   phloem   stomatal pore

waxy cuticle
upper epidermis
palisade mesophyll

spongy mesophyll

guard cell

lower epidermis

▶ *A cross-section of a leaf.*

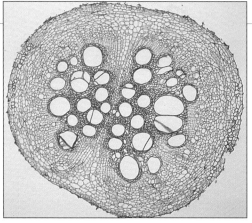

▲ *This section through a root shows the xylem and the phloem vessels. Phloem transports sugars around the plant.*

XYLEM VESSELS

There are also highly specialised cells which carry water from the roots all the way up to the leaves. These cells develop into tiny tubes, each cell joins with one below and one above to form a long continuous tube for the water to pass through. These cells are called **xylem** (pronounced 'zy-lem') **vessels**. They are special because as they develop, the inside of the cell dies and forms a hollow tube allowing the water to flow smoothly.

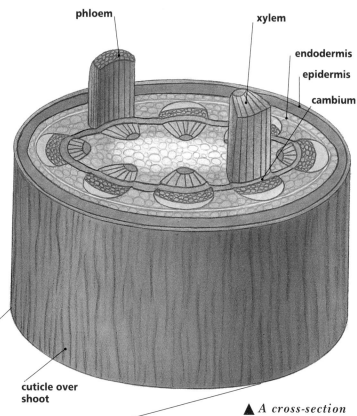

phloem · xylem · endodermis · epidermis · cambium

cuticle over shoot

cut end of shoot

▲ *A cross-section of a stem.*

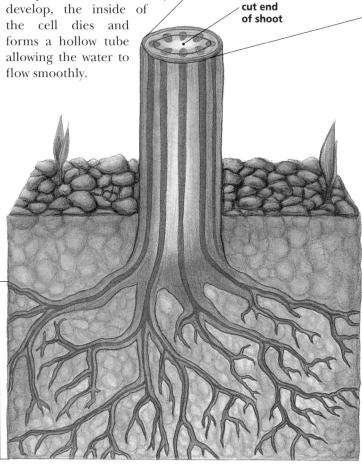

ROOT HAIR CELLS

To make sure that there is always a supply of water through the stem to the leaves, plants have a very special type of cell found only in the root. This cell produces a very long hair-like extension which stretches out between the particles of soil. If you have ever germinated peas or beans on blotting paper then you will have seen the wispy hair-like growths near the end of the root. These are hundreds of extensions formed from the **root hair cells** which line the outside of the root.

The long extensions have the effect of increasing the surface area of the tiny root cell many, many times. When thousands of these cells produce similar extensions, then the surface of the root is multiplied hundreds of times and makes the whole process of water uptake much more efficient.

■ *For more about plants see pp40–41.*

◄ *Because of the plant's extensive root system, water uptake is spread over a large surface area.*

FRICTIO

Q What have the following things got in common?

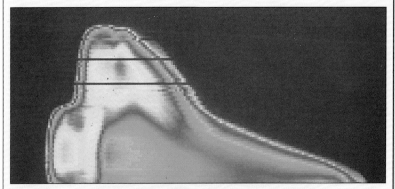

The heat pattern on the surface of the shuttle.

A car accelerating along a road.

Breaking the world record with a new design of bike.

A **FRICTION!**

The friction between the air and the outer surface of the space shuttle causes it to heat up as it re-enters the Earth's atmosphere.

The car accelerates because the wheels grip the road and the force of friction between the road and the wheels pushes the car forwards when the engine turns the wheels. If the wheels skid on the road due to ice or snow then there is little friction and the car does not move forwards.

The friction between the road surface and the wheels moves a bike forwards just like a car, but the friction between the bike and rider and the air puts an upper limit on the speed. If the drag of the air can be reduced the bike will go faster. Speed cyclists wear special clothes and helmets to help reduce the drag. They also crouch into a special position and even shave their legs!

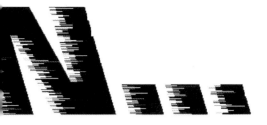

Friction is a **force**. It occurs when two things in contact move past each other. When solid objects are in contact, the force also occurs when the two surfaces try to move past each other, before they actually start to slide.

What causes the friction force?

If you look through a very powerful microscope at surfaces that seem smooth you see that they are actually quite rough.

When points from the different surfaces make contact the surfaces stick to each other. This causes the friction force when two surfaces are in contact and not sliding. When the surfaces start to slide the points break away from where they are joined and stick to new points. The continual breaking and joining causes the friction force when something is sliding.

How can friction be reduced?

Smoother surfaces have less friction. Try sliding a bean can on a rough plank of wood and compare the force needed with the force you need to push it on a smooth breadboard.

Rolling objects have less friction than sliding objects. You can see this easily with a bean can. It is much easier to roll it across a rough surface than it is to push it.

■ *For more about friction see p91.*

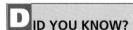

ID YOU KNOW?

Friction causes wasted energy in all machines! For example, about one-fifth of the energy used in a car engine is wasted by friction of the moving parts.

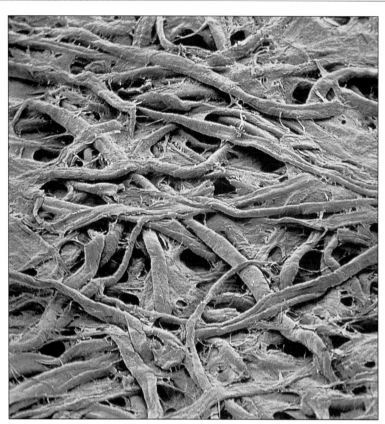

▲ *At a magnification of about 90×, the surface of a piece of paper does not look smooth. The fibres are from the wood pulp from which the paper is made.*

Friction is useful

You could not walk without friction! It is the friction force between your feet and the ground that pushes you forwards. Walking on wet ice when the friction force is very small is difficult.

Speed	Thinking distance	Braking distance
50 km/h	10 m	15 m
65 km/h	14 m	26 m
80 km/h	16 m	42 m
110 km/h	24 m	82 m

The friction between a car tyre and the road also provides the force that stops a car when the brakes are applied.

The stopping distances above are for a dry road with good tyres when the car does not skid. If the road is wet or the car skids the stopping distances are longer because the friction force is reduced.

ROCKETS & SATE

Sir Isaac Newton

Isaac Newton was the first person to describe that forces always come in pairs. The pairs act in opposite directions, and they act on different bodies. If you blow up a balloon and then let it go it will fly around the room. What makes the balloon move? Forces come in pairs; when the balloon pushes the air inside it backwards, the balloon itself gets pushed forwards.

Jet engines

Jet engines and rockets work on the same idea. The exhaust gases are pushed out of the back. Because forces come in pairs, this produces a forwards push on the rocket or jet. A jet engine needs to take in air as it moves along. A rocket does not take in anything – it already has all it needs inside it. It contains fuel and oxygen.

▼ *The front view of a jet engine. The fan blades are turned by a small core jet engine and produce the thrust.*

gases push rocket forwards

rocket pushes gases backwards

Rockets

The first rockets are thought to have been invented by the Chinese in about the 11th century. These were solid fuel rockets rather like firework rockets. Large rockets that could travel long distances were first built during the Second World War. In 1942, a team of German scientists led by Wernher von Braun developed the V2 rocket which was used to bomb London in the Second World War. After the war von Braun went to America. Here he led the team of scientists that developed the Saturn rockets that carried the Apollo Moon vehicle which landed on the Moon in 1969. In the early years of space flight the aim was to launch satellites. Then the aim shifted to launching vehicles into space and ensuring their safe return. The first space flight with a human on board was on 12 April 1961, when Yuri Gagarin flew round the Earth once.

Space rockets have to carry massive amounts of fuel and liquid oxygen. Their range of travel is greater if they are divided into stages. The Saturn V was a three-stage rocket. When the fuel in the first stage had been used up, the empty part of the rocket was cast away or jettisoned. As a result, the remaining sections were much lighter. This meant that the energy of the fuel was not used in accelerating empty sections of the rocket.

When a spacecraft returns from space and re-enters the Earth's atmosphere, it is travelling at a very high speed. The friction between the spacecraft and the atmosphere slows the craft down. In the process, the temperature of the outside surface of the spacecraft rises and can easily reach 1500°C

LLITES

on re-entry (five times as hot as a pizza oven!). It is important that the heat does not reach the crew inside. Spacecraft are designed with special materials that insulate the crew. Each of the surface tiles covering the NASA space shuttles is linked to a computer. This means that the individual temperature of each tile can be measured during re-entry.

The friction between fast-moving objects and the Earth's atmosphere is useful. The discarded sections of rockets falling back to Earth get so hot that they burn up in the atmosphere. So you need not worry about space junk dropping on your head. You may have seen these in the sky as they burn up – they appear as 'shooting stars'.

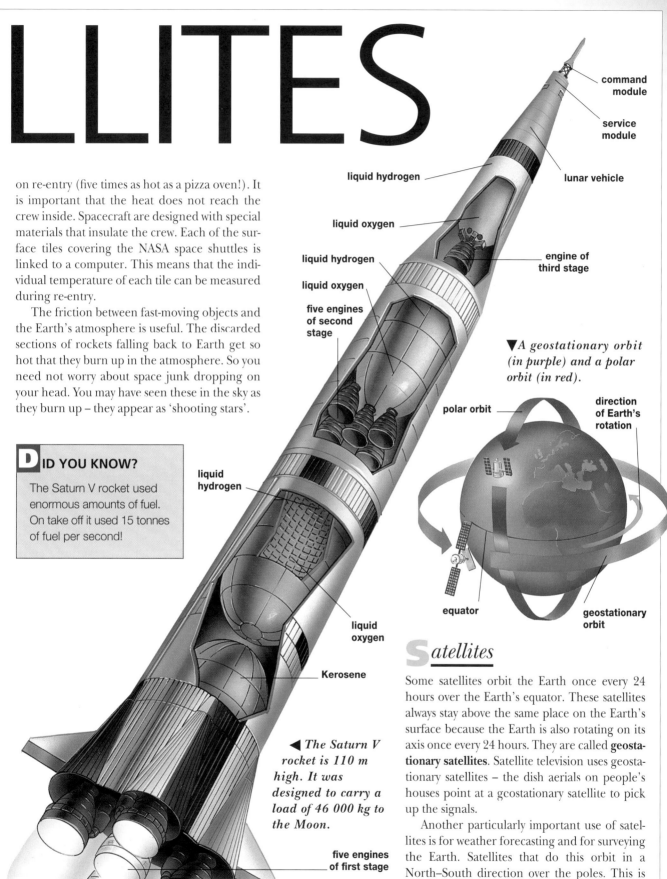

command module

service module

liquid hydrogen

lunar vehicle

liquid oxygen

liquid hydrogen

engine of third stage

liquid oxygen

five engines of second stage

DID YOU KNOW?

The Saturn V rocket used enormous amounts of fuel. On take off it used 15 tonnes of fuel per second!

liquid hydrogen

liquid oxygen

Kerosene

◀ *The Saturn V rocket is 110 m high. It was designed to carry a load of 46 000 kg to the Moon.*

five engines of first stage

▼*A geostationary orbit (in purple) and a polar orbit (in red).*

polar orbit

direction of Earth's rotation

equator

geostationary orbit

Satellites

Some satellites orbit the Earth once every 24 hours over the Earth's equator. These satellites always stay above the same place on the Earth's surface because the Earth is also rotating on its axis once every 24 hours. They are called **geostationary satellites**. Satellite television uses geostationary satellites – the dish aerials on people's houses point at a geostationary satellite to pick up the signals.

Another particularly important use of satellites is for weather forecasting and for surveying the Earth. Satellites that do this orbit in a North–South direction over the poles. This is called a **polar orbit**.

Newton AND

Isaac Newton was a great scientist. We still use his ideas about forces to predict the motion of objects. When he was only 24 he worked out the law that explained the motion of the planets and why objects fall to the Earth's surface.

Newton realised that all masses attract each other. The attraction is obvious when at least one of the masses is very large like the Earth. You can feel the pull of the Earth on you. We call it **weight**. Did you know that when you jump off a wall and the Earth pulls down, you are pulling the Earth up just as hard? So why do you think you don't notice the Earth moving?

Small masses attract each other, but the force is so small that it is very difficult to detect. The idea that all masses attract each other is called **Newton's Law of Gravitation**.

▼ *The force of attraction between two cricket balls when their centres are 15 cm apart is about 77 million millionths of a newton – not very much!*

S ir Isaac Newton (1643–1727) was born in Woolsthorpe, Lincolnshire. He went to study in Cambridge in 1661, but had to return home in 1665 to avoid catching the plague. It is thought that at this time he discovered the laws of mechanics, the law of gravity and the beginnings of mathematical calculus. He returned to Cambridge in 1667, and in 1669 became professor of mathematics. In 1686 he published a book The Mathematical Principles of Natural Philosophy *which explained his theories about the orbits of the planets and the Moon.*

Discovery of Neptune

Newton put his ideas about gravitation to the test in many ways. He predicted the motion of comets and explained why there are two tides a day. One of the most famous tests of his theories was in 1845.

The planets Mercury, Venus, Mars, Jupiter and Saturn are visible with the naked eye and have been observed by astronomers since ancient times. In 1781 the planet Uranus was discovered by the astronomer William Herschel, using a telescope. By the middle of the 19th century it was clear that the path of Uranus did not fit in with Newton's Law of Gravitation. So, either Newton was wrong or another planet was affecting the path. Scientists worked for years using Newton's laws to predict where the new planet could be found. Eventually, on 23 September 1846, it was observed and called Neptune.

In fact, Neptune had been observed 233 years earlier by Galileo, when he was studying the moons of Jupiter. Galileo did not realise he was observing a new planet – he thought that Neptune was a star – but he wrote down his observations.

■ *For more about Galileo see pp86–9.*

THE m**oo**n

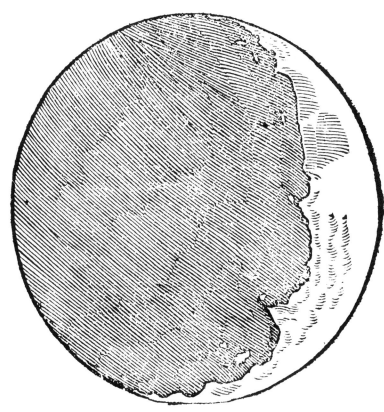

▲ *Galileo's drawing of the crescent moon in 1610. The Moon here is about 3½ days old with North at the top.*

The Moon's orbit

Isaac Newton used his theory of gravity to explain the Moon's orbit. His explanation was along the following lines (it works for any other **satellite**, too).

If you drop a stone it will fall straight downwards, towards the centre of the Earth. If you throw a stone sideways it will fall to the Earth but this time, because of the sideways motion, it will fall in a curve.

If you could throw a stone fast enough from a very high mountain (above the atmosphere) it would fall in a curve that followed the curve of the Earth's surface. If this happened the stone would never reach the Earth's surface. It would just continue to orbit the Earth. Your chance of doing this is nil! You would need to throw the stone at a speed of about 11 200 ms^{-1} – that is about ten times the speed of a bullet fired from a gun.

The Moon is continually falling towards the Earth. But, like the imaginary stone, it has sideways motion. It falls in a curve that follows the curve of the Earth's surface. That is, it never reaches the Earth. It orbits the Earth because there is a pull of gravity between it and the Earth.

■ *For more about the planets see pp86–9.*

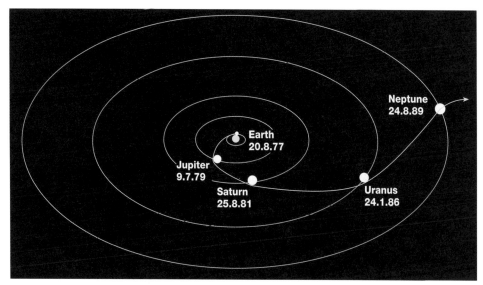

Neptune 24.8.89	
Earth 20.8.77	
Jupiter 9.7.79	
Saturn 25.8.81	Uranus 24.1.86

◀*Voyager 2 was flung out towards Uranus and Neptune by the gravitational attraction of Jupiter and Saturn.*

FLOATING

Most types of wood will float on water but some, like ebony, box and lignum vitae, will sink. A ball of modelling clay sinks in water, but if it is made into a boat shape it will float. In the same way a lump of iron will sink in water, but an iron ship will float.

▶ The boat and the float are floating, the fish has neutral buoyancy and the other objects have sunk.

Why do some things float while others sink?

When something is immersed in a liquid there is an upwards push called **upthrust** from the liquid on the object. Archimedes worked out that the size of the upwards push or upthrust from the liquid was equal to the weight of liquid pushed out of the way by the object. This idea is called **Archimedes' principle**.

Archimedes (c.287–212BC) was a Greek mathematician and inventor who lived in Syracuse, a town in Sicily. His work led him to make some important discoveries. He invented a rotating device for raising water or grain – the Archimedean screw. These are still used today to lift water.

▼ Submarines move to different depths by using Archimedes' principle.

▲ As the handle is turned, water is fed into the spiral screw. As the screw keeps moving water is brought up to a trough or reservoir at the top of the machine.

The well-known story about Archimedes says that one day when he got in the bath it overflowed! He jumped out and ran through town shouting 'Eureka' (Greek for 'I've found it'). He had realised that he could measure the volume of gold in the King's crown by putting it in a container of water and measuring the volume of the overflow.

Submarine floats

The ballast tanks are full of air and the valves are closed

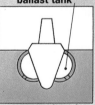

ballast tank

and SINKING

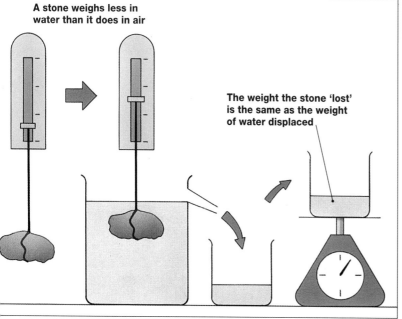

A stone weighs less in
water than it does in air

The weight the stone 'lost'
is the same as the weight
of water displaced

▲ *The upthrust equals the weight of
water displaced.*

Archimedes' principle
*When an object floats in a fluid, the
upwards force on the object is equal
to the weight of the fluid which is
displaced (pushed out of the way by
the object).*

D ID YOU KNOW?

Sharks don't have a swim bladder! They
have to keep swimming to prevent themselves sinking, even when they are asleep!
Their movement through the water produces upthrust, much like the movement
of a plane through the air keeps it up.
When the shark is swimming, the angle of
its body and fins produces additional
upthrusts that keep it afloat in the water.

▼ *Some fish have a swim bladder.
This is a bag of air inside their
bodies which gives them neutral
buoyancy. Their weight is exactly
balanced by the upwards force from
the water.*

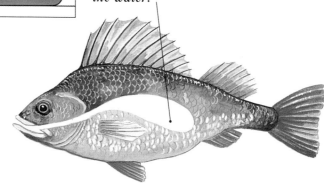

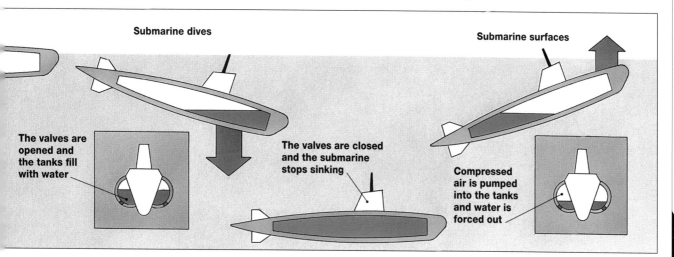

Submarine dives

Submarine surfaces

The valves are
opened and
the tanks fill
with water

The valves are closed
and the submarine
stops sinking

Compressed
air is pumped
into the tanks
and water is
forced out

FL⊗ATING

A **hydrometer** is a float, made of plastic or glass. To float it has to push its own weight of liquid out of the way. In a heavy liquid, like sugar syrup, it does not sink as far as it does in a lighter liquid like alcohol.

Brewers and winemakers use a hydrometer to check the level of alcohol in the brew. Alcoholic drinks are made by adding yeast to a solution of sugar. The yeast gradually **ferments** the sugar into alcohol. Sugar solution has a **density** higher than water. The more sugar there is in the solution, the higher the density will be. As the sugar is changed into alcohol the density falls. Alcohol is less dense than water. If a brewer knows how much sugar was put in the brew to start with then a measurement of density (using a hydrometer) will show how much alcohol has been made.

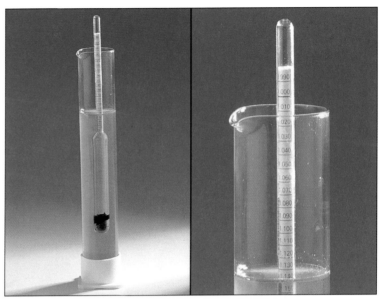

▲ *The scale on the hydrometer tells you how dense the liquid is. This liquid has a density of 1.14 g/cm³.*

WHALES AND ELEPHANTS

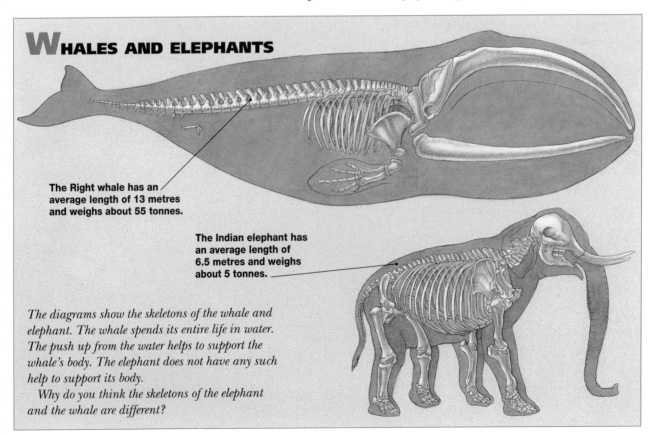

The Right whale has an average length of 13 metres and weighs about 55 tonnes.

The Indian elephant has an average length of 6.5 metres and weighs about 5 tonnes.

The diagrams show the skeletons of the whale and elephant. The whale spends its entire life in water. The push up from the water helps to support the whale's body. The elephant does not have any such help to support its body.

Why do you think the skeletons of the elephant and the whale are different?

and SINKING

Liquids are different!

If you do a fair comparison of how heavy different liquids are, you get results like these.

Substance	Density
Mercury	13.6 gcm^{-3}
Water	1.0 gcm^{-3}
Hydrochloric acid	1.2 gcm^{-3}
Olive oil	0.9 gcm^{-3}
Petrol	0.9 gcm^{-3}
Sea water	1.027 gcm^{-3}

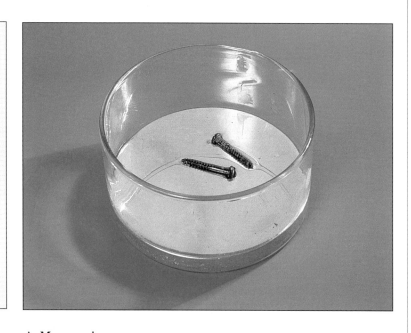

A *Cartesian diver*

Set up an eye dropper in a flexible plastic drinks bottle as shown. Part-fill it with water so that it just floats when the modelling clay is attached. Screw the top tight on to the bottle. Squeeze the bottle. What happens to the eye dropper? What happens to the size of the air bubble inside the eye dropper when you squeeze the bottle? Can you explain why the eye dropper behaves as it does?

The float you have made is called a 'Cartesian diver'. It was invented by René Descartes in the 17th century.

> **R**ené Descartes (1596–1650) was a French philosopher, mathematician and natural scientist. He invented analytical geometry and was the first philosopher to describe the Universe in terms of mind and matter. His Latin motto 'cogito, ergo sum' (I think, therefore I am) is famous. It means that because we have thoughts, we exist.

▲ *Mercury is a dense liquid metal. Steel screws will float on its surface.*

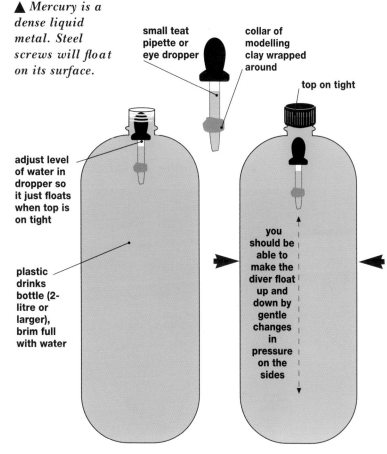

small teat pipette or eye dropper

collar of modelling clay wrapped around

top on tight

adjust level of water in dropper so it just floats when top is on tight

plastic drinks bottle (2-litre or larger), brim full with water

you should be able to make the diver float up and down by gentle changes in pressure on the sides

BRIDGES

People have always needed bridges. Even quite small streams can get in the way of the transport of goods. On our motorway system, bridges separate the motorway from other roads. Imagine what a motorway journey would be like if every bridge was replaced with a roundabout!

Beam bridge

The simplest type of bridge is a **beam** supported at each end. The weight of the beam and the **load** on it are forces acting downwards. These forces are balanced by upward forces acting where the supports meet the beam.

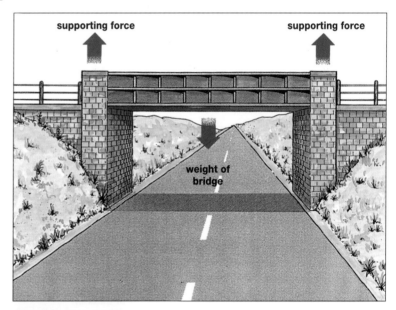

supporting force   supporting force

weight of bridge

▶ *A beam bridge.*

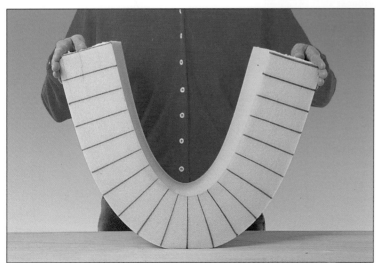

The beam of a simple bridge tends to bend, partly under its own weight and partly because of any load on it. The bending produces a **compression** force in the top of the beam and a **tension** force in the bottom. You can see the effect of these forces on the foam beam on the left.

There are bridges of this type on Dartmoor that date back to the Stone Age!

◀ *Vertical parallel lines were drawn on this foam beam before it was bent. You can see how the top side of 'the bend' is compressed and the underside is stretched (under tension).*

Cantilever bridge

A second type of bridge is the **cantilever** bridge. Two cantilevers and a beam supported between them can be used to provide a long span. The top of each cantilever will be in tension and the bottom will be in compression.

A famous example of this kind of bridge is the road bridge across the Firth of Forth. Here the middle section is suspended between the two cantilevers.

▶ *The Firth of Forth cantilever bridge was opened in 1890. Benjamin Baker was knighted for his design of this bridge.*

all the stones in the arch are being compressed

Arch bridges

Tension forces in some types of bridge can be a problem. When bridges are made from concrete, the concrete is **reinforced** with metal rods set in it. Without the rods the concrete would crack under tension. If a bridge is made from stones and mortar then tension forces will break the joints apart. The **arch** is a type of bridge that can be made so that there are no tension forces in it. With the correct shape of stones an arch can be made that does not need mortar.

Many variations of the arch are used in bridge building.

◀ *An arch bridge.*

Suspension bridges

Long bridges, with main spans over 600 m, use the **suspension** principle. High towers support cables and the cables support a beam.

■ *For more about forces see pp28–9.*

▶ *The Golden Gate bridge under construction.*

D ID YOU KNOW?

A famous and unusual bridge was built at Bridgewater on the Manchester Ship Canal to carry one canal over another.

Plant adaptat

Plants show all kinds of adaptations which help them survive in the places they live. Some of the plants which are adapted best are those which live in very hot and dry climates like deserts.

▶ *Looking down on the root system of a cactus.*

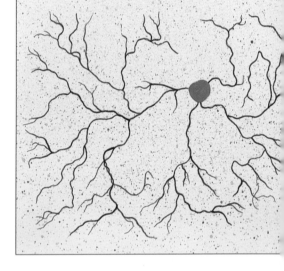

Life cycle

In some regions of semi-desert, like some areas of the United States of America, there is a short rainy season followed by a long drought. In order to survive, the plants must grow and produce seeds quickly. One example of this life cycle is the Californian 'poppy'. As soon as the rain falls, the seeds **germinate** and grow into plants. The plants flower and the flowers form seeds all before the ground becomes totally dry once more. This all happens in a matter of two to three weeks! The seeds remain in the ground until the next rainy season. So the plant is **adapted** to grow rapidly and complete its life cycle in a very short time.

The cactus

Probably the most famous desert plant is the cactus. The cactus is adapted to life in the desert because it cuts down water loss. Even in the high desert temperatures the cactus holds on to the water it absorbed during the last rainy period. Look at the diagram of the root network in a common cactus plant. The roots are shallow but very extensive, so that if rain comes the water can be absorbed quickly over a wide area.

The real trick to the survival of the cactus is its stem. The stem is thick, there are no leaves (most plants lose lots of water from their leaves) and there is a thick outside layer. The shape of the cactus also helps to cut down water loss because the cactus has a small surface area compared with its bulk.

A calculation has shown that the speed of water loss from a cactus plant compared with a plant living in non-desert conditions may be up to one thousand times slower!

In an investigation, the giant cactus (carnegia) was kept in a laboratory for six years without ever being watered and after this time it had lost only about one-third of its original water content.

ions

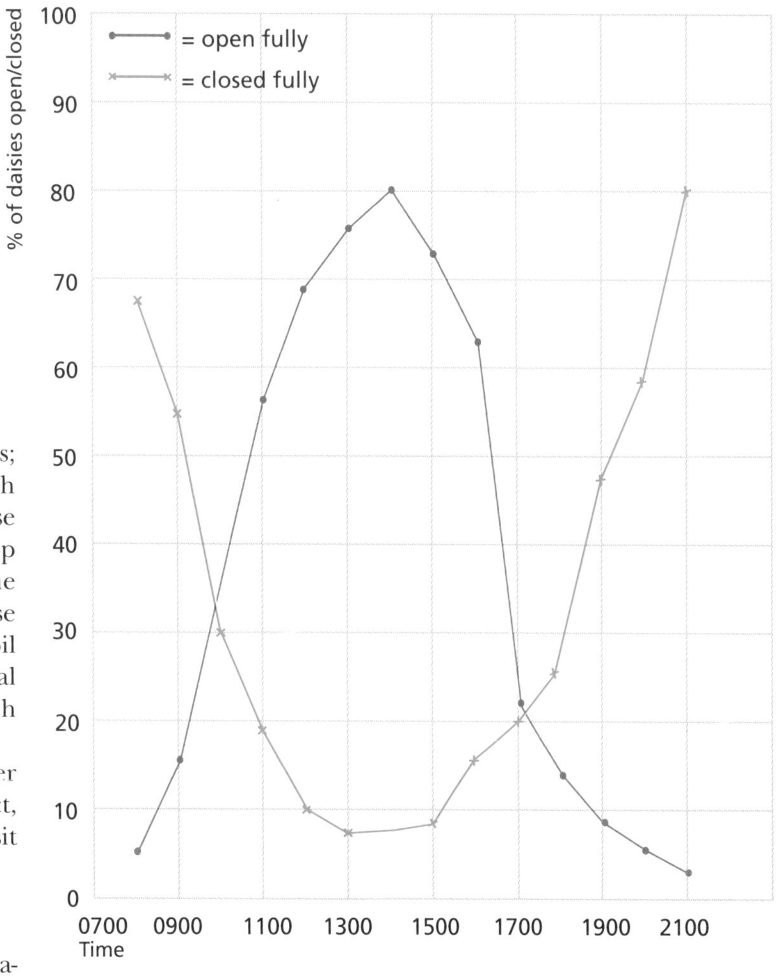

% of daisies open/closed

- ● = open fully
- ✕ = closed fully

Time: 0700 0900 1100 1300 1500 1700 1900 2100

SEASONAL ADAPTATIONS

Many plants change with different seasons; again these are often adaptations which help them to survive. **Deciduous** trees lose their leaves in autumn. The plants stop growing and 'shut down' activity during the cold winter months. This is mainly because water is difficult to absorb from the soil during cold weather, also the chemical activity in the leaf of the plant is much slower in the colder conditions.

Insect-pollinated plants must flower when there arc lots of insects about. In fact, the insects and the flowers that they visit depend on each other.

DIURNAL ADAPTATIONS

There are certain flowers such as the clematis which open only at night. This is often because the insect, which visits this flower for food, is a night-flying moth.

This kind of opening and closing each 24 hours is known as a **diurnal** pattern or rhythm. Another interesting example of this is with the common daisy. The graph above shows the pattern of opening and closing during the day. The daisy flowers open in the morning, remain open and then close in the evcning. Notice that many

▼ *A large emerald moth visits the clematis flower at night.*

of the daisies open at the same time of day.

The small pores on the leaves (stomatal pores) also show a diurnal pattern. The pores tend to open during the day and close at night. The opening of the pores during the day allows gases to enter and leave the leaf, including water vapour. The water vapour evaporates from the leaf and this has the effect of drawing water up the stem from the roots. The need for water decreases as evening and night-time draws in and so the supply of water slows down at night as the pores close.

TRACKING SUNLIGHT

Another adaptation which can be secn in many plants, particularly if they are are on window sills, is the way in which leaves turn to the sunlight as it moves around during the day. The leaves seem to track the Sun across the sky. This is an obvious advantage, because as the leaf faces the Sun it can absorb the maximum amount of light.

Photosynthesis

Plants have the ability to make complicated substances like carbohydrates (e.g. starch) from very simple raw materials. This chemical reaction is called **photosynthesis**, *and is summarised in the following way:*

Water	+	Carbon dioxide	Sunlight → Chlorophyll	Sugar	+	Oxygen
$6H_2O$	+	$6CO_2$		$C_6H_{12}O_6$	+	$6O_2$

Green plants **photosynthesise**. To do this, plants must absorb sunlight and must contain the green pigment called **chlorophyll**. Once the plant has made carbohydrates it can then go further and make lots of other important nutrients like proteins, fats and a whole range of special substances, including some which we call vitamins.

Plants need minerals

To make proteins and vitamins and all the other substances which plants contain, a range of **minerals** is needed. The plant absorbs these from the soil by root hair cells. All proteins contain the elements carbon (C), hydrogen (H), oxygen (O), nitrogen (N) and sulphur (S). The carbon, hydrogen and oxygen can be taken from the carbon dioxide and the water. The nitrogen comes from **nitrates** (NO_3^-) and the sulphur comes from **sulphates** (SO_4^{2-}), both are present in fertile soils. Plants also need a whole range of other minerals such as iron and magnesium. The green substance found in plant cells, chlorophyll, is a complicated substance vital for photosynthesis. It contains magnesium and if the plant can't get magnesium from the soil then the plant is unable to grow properly. Sometimes potted plants begin to look

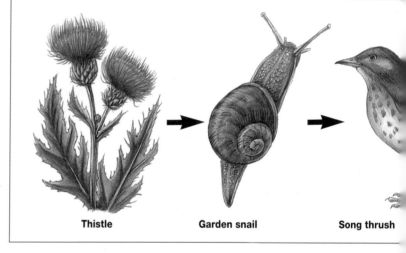

Thistle   **Garden snail**   **Song thrush**

Blackberries

unhealthy, having yellow leaves. This may be because the soil in the pot is running out of certain vital minerals which the plant needs.

■ *For more about plant cells see pp26–7.*

and food chains

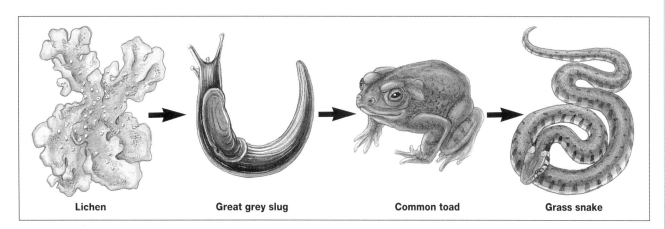

Lichen	**Great grey slug**	**Common toad**	**Grass snake**

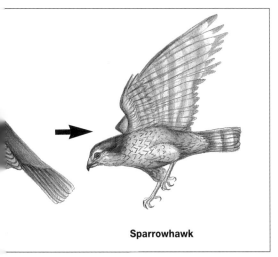

Sparrowhawk

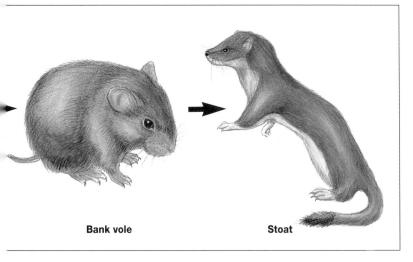

Bank vole   **Stoat**

Food chains

Because plants are the only living organisms that can make complicated nutrients from simple raw materials they are called **producers**. This means that they produce the nutrients which feed animals. The animals are called **consumers** because they consume the food.

We can see this if we study the **food chain** below. When a vole eats blackberries then a stoat eats the vole this is called a food chain. A number of food chains are shown on this page.

The animals which feed off the plants are called **herbivores** or 1st consumers. Animals which feed off other animals are called **carnivores**, and these may be 2nd or 3rd or 4th consumers, depending on where they come in the chain.

Photosynthesis

Food webs

In nature food chains may merge together, this is called a **food web**. An example of a food web is given on the right.

There are certain important patterns which we see when we look at the producers and consumers in food chains and webs.

- Food chains/webs usually begin with a plant, or a part of a plant.
- The animals at the end of a food chain are often larger than the animals near the start.
- The number or total mass of living organisms decreases as you get further away from the plant producers.

These patterns are connected with **energy**. As far as living organisms are concerned food is energy, or at least food energy can be transferred into movement energy, heat energy, electrical energy, and so on.

When plants make food they transform the energy from the Sun into food (energy stored in nutrients like proteins and carbohydrates and fats, etc.). At the start of the food chain there is enough energy for the plant to use and enough to feed a large number of herbivores (1st consumers). After two or three transfers of this energy there is only enough to support a small number of carnivores.

WHAT HAPPENS TO THE ENERGY?

The energy does not 'disappear'. It is transformed into a form which animals can't use. For example if a cow eats grass, the cow may eat only the top part of the plant. All the roots, which may contain lots of food energy in the form of nutrients, may stay under the soil. There may also be some part of the plant's stem or leaves which the cow can't digest. This will pass straight through the ców and end up in cow manure! Also the plant uses the food which it makes for itself. The animal can get only a part of the nutrients stored in the plant at the time that it actually eats the plant. Therefore the cow can get only a small quantity of the energy which that plant has trapped.

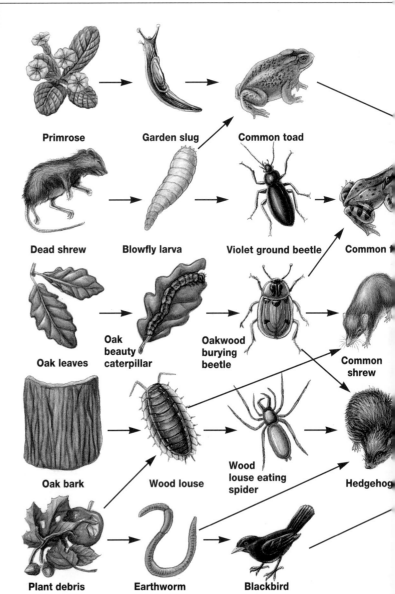

Primrose → Garden slug → Common toad

Dead shrew → Blowfly larva → Violet ground beetle → Common f

Oak leaves → Oak beauty caterpillar → Oakwood burying beetle → Common shrew

Oak bark → Wood louse → Wood louse eating spider → Hedgehog

Plant debris → Earthworm → Blackbird

and food webs

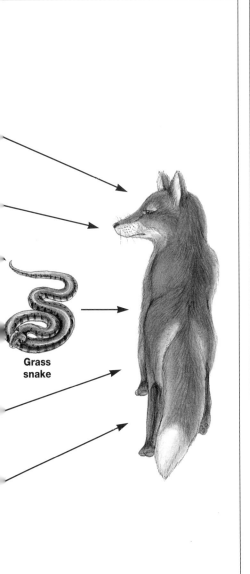

Grass snake

▲ *A woodland food web.*

PYRAMIDS OF NUMBERS/BIOMASS

If the numbers of plants and animals at each stage in a food chain are counted and drawn on a chart we get a pattern. The pattern looks very like a pyramid as shown below:

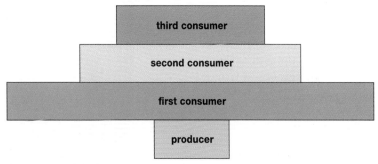

| third consumer |
| second consumer |
| first consumer |
| producer |

▲ *A pyramid of numbers.*

A more reliable measurement is to count the mass of living organisms at a particular level. This gets over the problem of counting a large tree as one organism. The same sort of pattern is produced and is called a pyramid of biomass. These patterns show that the total amount of food/energy present at each level reduces dramatically as you move up the food chain.

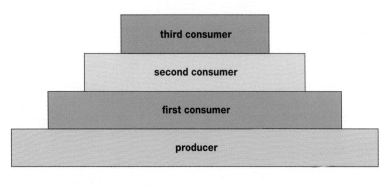

| third consumer |
| second consumer |
| first consumer |
| producer |

▲ *A pyramid of biomass.*

ENERGY *that never runs out*

We use a lot of energy! For example, all the processes used to make just one can for a fizzy drink use up to 5 000 000 J (5 MJ). When a car uses a litre of petrol it transfers about 20 000 000 joules (20 MJ) from **stored energy** in the fuel to **kinetic energy**; the engine also gets hot. A typical house in western Europe will transfer about 17 000 000 000 J (= 17 000 MJ = 17 GJ) of energy a year to heat and light. Most of this energy comes from oil, coal and natural gas. Eventually, the energy spreads out into the environment.

Our supplies of oil and natural gas are running low. Reserves of coal may last about 300 years but oil and natural gas may last only for about 30 years. We need to develop and use sources of energy that will not run out – **renewable energy sources**.

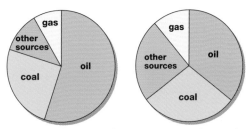

▲ *Pie charts showing the proportions of fuels used in 1980, and an estimate of the proportions proportions used in 2000.*

The Sun

Enormous amounts of energy are transferred from the Sun to the Earth – about 10 000 000 000 000 000 000 000 J *each day*! We transfer very little of this to do useful jobs. Still, you may have seen 'solar panels' on the roofs of some houses. These transfer the Sun's energy to water, to run the hot water system in the house. In some sunny parts of the world there are power stations that run on solar energy; this can be transferred to electricity using **solar cells**. Small solar cells are used in calculators and bigger ones are used in satellites.

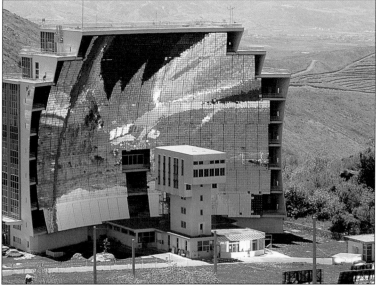

Wind

The energy in the wind originally comes from the Sun. Wind is the movement of great masses of air, which is caused by heat from the Sun. Sailing ships use the wind for their energy source, as did the windmills that ground corn. Modern windmills can transfer the energy of the wind into an electric current. Wind will not run out, unlike coal, but it can be unreliable. The wind blows only very little on some days. You would need a lot of windmills to replace a big power station!

▲ *The parabolic reflector in the Eastern Pyrenees, France. In front of the reflector, 63 flat mirrors (in the corner of the picture) automatically track the motion of the Sun. They reflect the radiation on to the large reflector. This concentrates the Sun's rays on to a dark coated furnace. Temperatures of 3800°C can be reached in the furnace.*

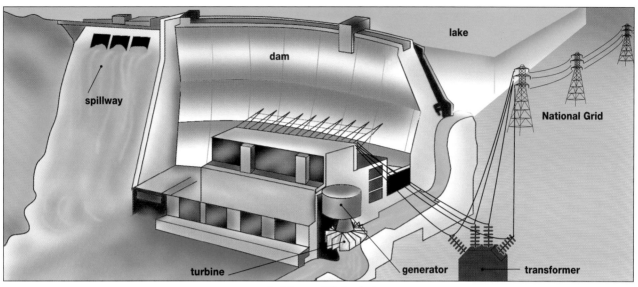

▲ *Most of Britain's hydroelectric power is produced in Scotland.*

Hydroelectricity

A large store of water can be collected behind a dam built across a river at a suitable point. The water is released so that it flows through a turbine connected to a generator; the energy of the falling water is transferred into an electric current. This type of electricity production is called **hydroelectric power**. Nearly 25 per cent of the world's electricity is produced by hydroelectric power stations.

In Scandinavia the shape of the land is particularly suitable for building hydroelectric power stations because there are lots of steep valleys with rivers flowing through them. In Norway, for example, most of the electricity is produced in these stations. Although hydroelectricity itself does not cause pollution, the large artificial lake formed behind a dam destroys much of the local plant and animal life. There is opposition to building more hydroelectric power stations in Sweden, because of the damage to the countryside.

■ *For more about water issues see pp56–9.*

Geothermal energy

The middle of the Earth is very hot. In some places the temperature at a depth of about 8 km is as high as 200 °C. In New Zealand and many other places there are springs that are hot because the water comes from deep inside the Earth. If water is pumped down very deep **boreholes**, it will be hot when it comes back to the surface. In Iceland, water from hot springs is used to heat houses and greenhouses. In some places the water emerges from the ground as steam. It is so hot that it can be used directly in power stations.

▶ *Energy is transferred from the hot rocks to the water.*

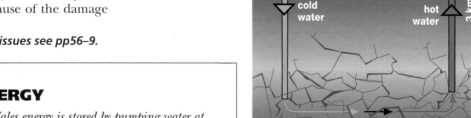

the water soaks through the cracks in the rocks

STORING ENERGY

At Dinorwic in North Wales energy is stored by pumping water at night, when demand for electricity is low, into a high reservoir. When extra electricity is needed during the day, this water is allowed to run back down through turbines. The turbines drive generators which produce an electric current. This is an example of a hydroelectric pumped storage scheme.

ENERGY *that never runs out*

Tides

The Moon moving round the Earth causes the sea tides. In some parts of the world large dams have been built across **estuaries**. The estuary fills with water at high tide and the water is trapped behind the dam when the tide drops. The trapped water is allowed to flow through channels back to the sea. As it does it turns **turbines**. These turn **generators** which transfer the stored energy into an electric current. The tidal power station on the Rance estuary at St Malo in France generates 240 MW ($= 240\ 000\ 000\ \mathrm{Js^{-1}}$).

■ *For more about generators see pp128–9.*

Waves

The wind blows on the sea and creates waves. The energy from waves can be transferred into an electric current by specially designed floats that move up and down on the surface of the sea.

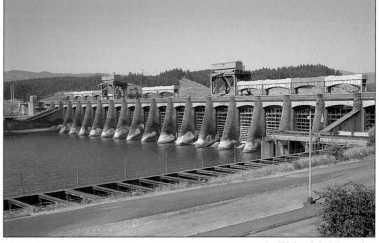

▲ *This tidal barrier is in Oregon, USA.*

▼ *As the floats bob up and down, the energy from their movement is used to generate electricity.*

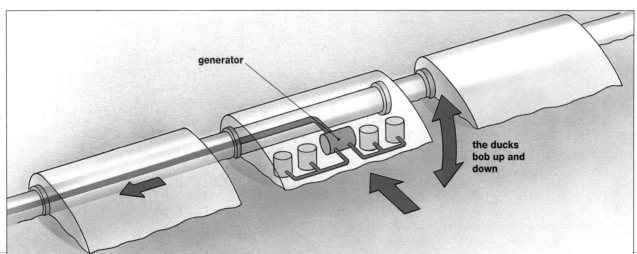

generator

the ducks bob up and down

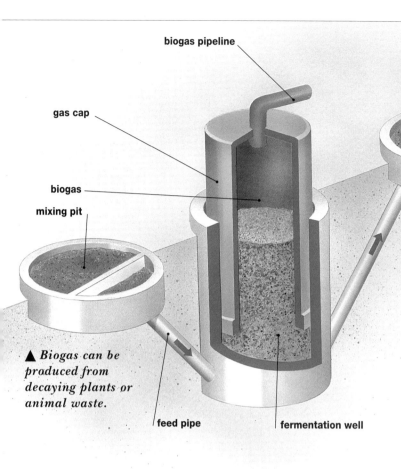

biogas pipeline

slurry tank

gas cap

biogas

mixing pit

▲ *Biogas can be produced from decaying plants or animal waste.*

feed pipe

fermentation well

Energy from biomass

Energy from the Sun is stored in plants as they grow. This is the energy we transfer when we burn wood. When dead plants rot under certain conditions they release a gas called **methane**. Methane is a fuel – it is the main ingredient of natural gas. If rotting plants are kept in a closed tank a steady supply of methane is produced. This can be piped off and burned, just like natural gas, so transferring some of the stored energy of the Sun to heating.

The unit of energy is named after the English scientist James Prescott Joule (1818–89). He was born on Christmas Eve 1818 in Salford and worked in Manchester. Joule was the son of a brewer and he inherited the family business. He did not have a university degree, and his first scientific paper was turned down by the Royal Society. This did not surprise Joule as he was from what was considered then to be an unfashionable northern town, and the famous scientists of the day did not know him. To quote his own words: 'I was not surprised. I could imagine those gentlemen in London sitting round a table and saying to each other, "What good can come out of a town where they dine in the middle of the day?"'

Joule studied science as a hobby. The paper that the Royal Society refused to publish in 1840 contained the important connection between the work done in turning an electric generator and the heat produced by the electric current flowing in the wires. This work was published in the Philosophical Magazine in 1843. He also put forward the idea that energy cannot be created or destroyed – it can only be transferred from one form to another. Above all, Joule was a scientist who used experiment and observations to put ideas to the test. One of his most famous experiments showed you that if you stir water then you increase its temperature.

NUCLEAR

What is nuclear fuel?

A fuel is something that produces heat when it is treated in a certain way. Most fuels give out heat when they burn. One special type of fuel, called **nuclear fuel** gives out heat without burning. All you have to do is put enough of the fuel in a small space and it gets very hot indeed.

Types of fuel

Fossil fuels	natural gas
	petroleum
	coal
	peat
	coke
Organic fuels	wood
	waste materials
Nuclear fuels	uranium
	plutonium

Nuclear fuel is made of **atoms** that are very large and **unstable**. Sometimes one of the atoms splits up into two smaller, different, atoms. It does this to become more stable. When an atom splits to become more stable a lot of energy is released and the block of substance it is in gets hotter. Nuclear fuel is made from purified **uranium** or **plutonium**. These substances are purified so that they will release a lot of heat in the right situation. One of the common nuclear fuels is called uranium 235.

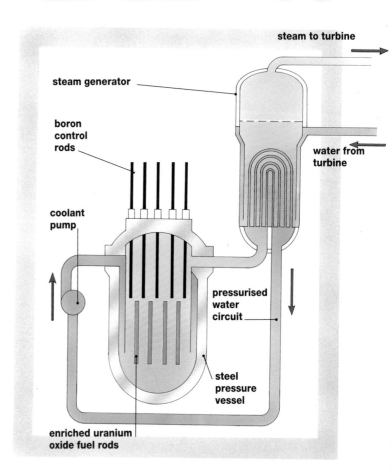

steam to turbine

steam generator

boron control rods

coolant pump

water from turbine

pressurised water circuit

steel pressure vessel

enriched uranium oxide fuel rods

How does a nuclear power station work?

A nuclear power station uses a nuclear reactor to produce heat and then uses this heat to produce steam. The steam is used to drive turbines which turn generators to make electricity. The only difference between a coal-fired power station and a nuclear power station is the source of heat. The rest of the process is the same.

■ *For more about power stations see* *pp128–9.*

▲ *A nuclear reactor uses the energy transferred in a nuclear reaction to heat the water to steam.*

energy

Why can nuclear fuel be dangerous?

Uranium and plutonium are **radioactive**. This means that like all the other substances that we call radioactive, they give off tiny invisible particles and waves that can harm living things. Some radioactive substances are very useful even though they are dangerous. All radioactive substances must be handled with care. Radioactivity occurs all around us at a very low level called the **background level**. We must be careful, however, that our use of very radioactive materials in nuclear power stations, in some branches of medicine and in industry in general does not increase the background level to a dangerous one.

HOW MUCH ENERGY IS RELEASED BY URANIUM?

1 g of uranium is about the size of a dressmaking pin. It contains about 2500 million million million atoms! Splitting all these atoms releases about as much energy as burning 500 gallons of oil. Scaling that up means that 1 kg of uranium can release as much energy as burning about 3000 million kg of coal!

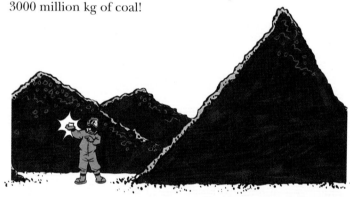

▶ *Sellafield nuclear power station and reprocessing plant in Cumbria. The dome used to house an Advanced Gas-Cooled Reactor (AGR) which operated from 1963 to 1981.*

Is it worth

Unfortunately, as with most industries, the nuclear power industry produces waste. As this waste can be radioactive we have to be very careful how we deal with it. The waste is classed as **low-level** *if it is not very radioactive,* **intermediate level** *if it is quite radioactive and* **high-level** *if it is very radioactive.*

What can be done with the waste?

The basic ideas used to get rid of radioactive waste are:

containment – wrap the waste up to stop the radiation reaching living things;

dispersal – dilute the waste so the concentration is so low that it is considered safe.

The nuclear industry tries to manage its waste so that:

- Whenever anyone is exposed to radiation, the benefit is greater than the harm;
- Any exposure to radiation is as low as can be achieved;
- Doses of radiation received by people do not exceed recommended levels;
- There is a minimum impact on future generations;
- The natural environment is preserved.

Not everyone would agree that these targets are met. However, the nuclear industry quotes figures like those above in its defence.

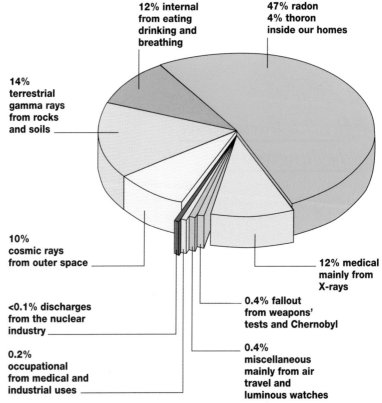

12% internal from eating drinking and breathing

47% radon 4% thoron inside our homes

14% terrestrial gamma rays from rocks and soils

10% cosmic rays from outer space

<0.1% discharges from the nuclear industry

0.2% occupational from medical and industrial uses

12% medical mainly from X-rays

0.4% fallout from weapons' tests and Chernobyl

0.4% miscellaneous mainly from air travel and luminous watches

▲ *Flying for one hour at a typical altitude exposes an air passenger to four times as much radiation as he/she receives from the entire nuclear industry in a year.*

▼ *Low-level radioactive waste being stored at British Nuclear Fuels' Drigg waste disposal site.*

Some examples of waste management

LOW-LEVEL WASTE

Examples of low-level solid waste are used laboratory equipment and old protective clothing. In Britain most of this type of material is disposed of at a 120-hectare (ha) site that is fenced off at Drigg near Sellafield in Cumbria. We produce between 25 000 and 40 000 m^3 of this waste each year. It is estimated that there is enough space at Drigg to last as a storage site until at least the year 2000.

Some low-level waste could be dumped at sea. The idea is that the waste is cast in concrete and sealed in drums before

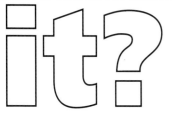

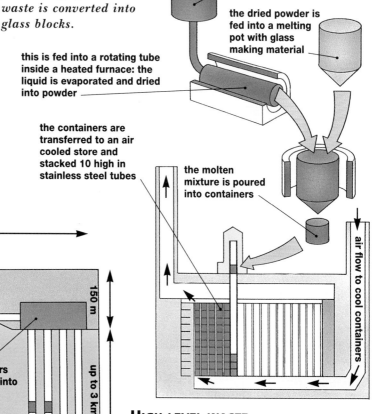

▶ *How highly radioactive waste is converted into glass blocks.*

highly active liquid waste

the dried powder is fed into a melting pot with glass making material

this is fed into a rotating tube inside a heated furnace: the liquid is evaporated and dried into powder

the molten mixture is poured into containers

the containers are transferred to an air cooled store and stacked 10 high in stainless steel tubes

air flow to cool containers

sinking to the sea bed. If the waste has a short **half-life** then it would be relatively harmless by the time the drum and concrete break up. Then, the radioactive material would be dispersed and diluted in the sea. However, the full effect of this type of disposal on marine life is not yet known.

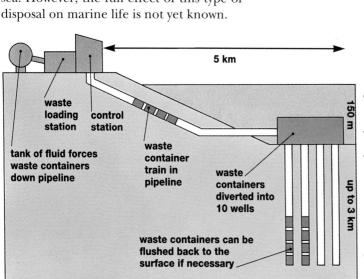

5 km

waste loading station

control station

tank of fluid forces waste containers down pipeline

waste container train in pipeline

waste containers diverted into 10 wells

150 m

up to 3 km

waste containers can be flushed back to the surface if necessary

INTERMEDIATE-LEVEL WASTE

Intermediate-level waste consists of things like the filters used to clean the gases and liquids, the scrap metal from the walls of the **fuel elements** and other left-over bits from the nuclear fuel. This waste is stored at places like the Sellafield reprocessing plant in Cumbria. It can be treated so that most of the radioactive material is extracted as high-level waste and the bulk of the material is then low-level waste that can be disposed of in the ways mentioned above. There are plans to build a deep **repository** for this waste and for some of the low-level waste. The possible site for this may be Dounrey in the north of Scotland or Sellafield.

When radioactive material is buried, it should be buried deep in the ground where water will not seep through it. Otherwise radioactive substances could be carried to the surface and into the food chains.

▲ *Storing low-level waste underground.*

▼ *The proposed underground storage method for intermediate-level waste.*

HIGH-LEVEL WASTE

High-level wastes can be stored provided they are cooled down and that care is taken to seal the radiation in.

The plan is to mix the waste with molten glass and cast it into blocks. These can then be buried deep in the ground away from areas where there is a risk of earthquakes. This is shown in the diagram above.

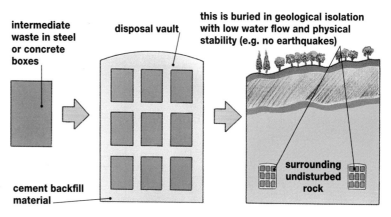

intermediate waste in steel or concrete boxes

disposal vault

this is buried in geological isolation with low water flow and physical stability (e.g. no earthquakes)

surrounding undisturbed rock

cement backfill material

Is it worth

The arguments for and against the nuclear industry are not simple. It is certainly true that our need for sources of energy has increased incredibly over the last 150 years and that the present known reserves of fossil fuel will not last long into the future.

We need to conserve energy and to use alternative sources. Whether the vast store of energy available from nuclear fuel is worth the risk depends on how you view some of the arguments below. Some well-informed people say that there is negligible risk associated with the nuclear industry. Others, equally well informed, point to the accidents that have happened at Windscale (Sellafield, Britain 1957), Three Mile Island (USA 1979) and Chernobyl (former USSR 1986) and say that the only safe level of radiation is none at all. Below are some of the arguments for and against using nuclear fuel. You will need to find out more about them before you start to make up your own mind.

Argument 1: The demand

The demand for energy is increasing. We have to meet it to maintain our comfortable lifestyle. We need nuclear power because our reserves of fossil fuels are running out. Large unmined reserves of uranium ore exist but alternative energy sources have still to be developed on a large scale.

Why not cut the demand? We should put our efforts into using non-nuclear energy efficiently. If we invested the money we put into the nuclear industry we would soon have developed alternative energy sources to meet our needs.

2 Nuclear power is cheap.

3 We have learnt from past mistakes – a major nuclear accident cannot happen again.

1 We need nuclear power because our reserves of fossil fuels are running out.

4 Toxic waste from conventional power stations is more dangerous than nuclear waste.

it?

Argument 2: The cost

It's cheap. Nuclear power stations produce electricity much more cheaply than other types of power station.

It depends how you count the cost. Some people are still suffering from the effects of one disaster in Russia at Chernobyl. If research into energy from the wind, the tides, the waves or the rivers was given as much priority as nuclear fuel then they could provide a lot of energy safely and cheaply!

Argument 3: Safety

The nuclear industry is very safe. There are fewer deaths per 1000 workers than in the coal mining industry. We have learnt from past mistakes at Windscale, Three Mile Island and Chernobyl. They could never happen again.

The risk is always there. You cannot totally eliminate human error. The Chernobyl accident had a varying effect on all living things from Ireland, across all of Europe and Scandinavia and deep into Russia as far as the Caspian Sea. Our own nuclear industry may not be blameless. Some studies have shown a higher incidence of babies with blood cancer and an increased number of Downs Syndrome children near some of our nuclear industrial establishments. Could there be a connection with the nuclear industry?

Argument 4: Toxic waste

There is a lot of waste produced by conventional power stations in terms of toxic chemicals and gases that cause acid rain and the greenhouse effect. Although this waste is not radioactive, it is dangerous because there is a lot more of it and it is not disposed of as safely as the small amount of radioactive waste produced by the nuclear industry.

No matter how dangerous the waste from conventional power, the high-level waste from nuclear power can be more dangerous because it stays radioactive for hundreds of years. We could put more work into cleaning up conventional power stations and developing clean sources of energy like the wind.

There are lots of other arguments for and against the nuclear industry. If you research the underlying facts, you will discover that they are not as simple as they first appear.

3 The risk is always there – and what about human error?

2 The effects of nuclear accidents are very costly in terms of both safety and money.

4 Nuclear power waste stays radioactive for hundreds of years.

1 We should invest money in ways of using non-nuclear energy efficiently.

BAN NUCLEAR POWER

WATER

Human activity can have catastrophic effects on the water cycle. For example, increased levels of the gases, in particular carbon dioxide, produced when we use fossil fuels (petrol, oil, coal natural gas) may cause the atmosphere to warm up. Gases such as carbon dioxide act like the glass of a greenhouse allowing the radiant heat from the Sun through and then trapping it.

This natural effect is called the **greenhouse effect** and keeps the Earth warm. However, if this effect is increased the extra increase in temperature could lead to the melting of all the ice on the Earth. If so, there will be more water in the sea, so the level of the sea may rise. This would change the coastlines of the world.

▶ *The light from the Sun enters the greenhouse as short wavelength infra-red. The plants and soil inside the greenhouse warm up and emit longer wavelength infra-red which is trapped inside the greenhouse.*

short wavelength infra-red

long wavelength infra-red

short wavelength infra-red from Sun

atmosphere

long wavelength infra-red from Earth stays trapped

Earth

◀ *Gases like carbon dioxide in the Earth's atmosphere act in the same way as the glass.*

ACID RAIN

▲ *This Norway Spruce forest is dying as a result of acid rain*

The same gases are also responsible for producing acid rain. *The waste gases produced by factories, power stations and cars rise into the air and react with the rainwater. Rain is normally slightly acidic, but this reaction makes it even more acidic. This rain is known as acid rain. The wind can carry the acid gases for long distances, and so acid rain can often fall far from the source of the gases.*

Animal and plant life are threatened by acid rain as the rain accumulates in lakes, rivers and soil increasing their acidity. You can see the effect of acid rain closer to home if you look at the erosion of buildings in some towns and cities.

issues

Strains on fresh water supplies

In some parts of the world there is not enough rainwater for growing crops, so water is supplied to fields from lakes and rivers by **irrigation** channels. In some places this irrigation can cause problems. The Aral Sea in Soviet Central Asia was once the fourth largest lake in the world. However, now it is only about the sixth largest: it has shrunk by nearly one-half its original size. This has happened because the main rivers which fed the giant lake are being used for irrigation. This has affected the climate around the lake. At places up to 100 km away, the summers are hotter, shorter and drier and the winters are longer and colder. Other effects include a decline in the wildlife of the region. Twenty

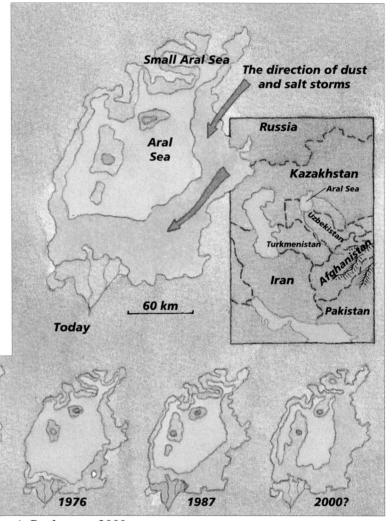

The changing profile

years ago there were at least 24 different species of fish in the lake, but now there are only 4 species left. Four-fifths of the forest that once surrounded the lake has disappeared affecting the animals that lived there.

Pollution

In the world there are many problems with water. In some countries there isn't enough; in others streams, rivers and the sea are used as dustbins: rubbish and waste are

▲ *By the year 2000 it is anticipated that the volume of the Aral Sea will be one-tenth of its volume in 1960.*

thrown into them. In North America some of the Great Lakes are being severely polluted by chemicals which have been allowed to leak into the lakes for years. Many of these chemicals are extremely poisonous and have killed off plants and animals in the lakes. Some fishermen in the North Sea find that their catches are decreasing. They also find an increasing number of fish which have damaged skins and sores. Many fishermen think that this is because pollution is poisoning the sea.

WHAT ARE WE DOING TO OUR WATER?

The areas of this planet which are covered by water are some of the richest as far as life is concerned. The seas, rivers, lakes and streams can contain a huge variety of life.

Fresh water and sea water both contain microscopic plants. These plants, called **plankton**, are very important to the rest of the life in the water. Small animals feed off these plankton, then bigger animals feed off them, and so on. Plants are also important in water because they help to keep the amount of oxygen in the water high. This is important because all the animals which live in water, from the smallest shrimp to the largest fish, need oxygen.

The numbers of microscopic plants, larger water plants and animals in any sea or river or lake are in a delicate balance. If this balance is upset, the plants and animals may be able to adjust themselves so that a new balance is achieved. Occasionally the balance can be upset and completely lost. The life in the water may recover but in severe cases the life in the water may be completely destroyed!

Eutrophication

We can see how delicate the balance is in rivers and seas by looking at the problem of **eutrophication** (pronounced 'you-troff-i-kayshon'). This word is used to describe a sample of water which has too many nutrients in it, and this causes the microscopic plants to grow and grow.

WHAT CAUSES EUTROPHICATION?

Modern farming uses fertilisers, and these chemicals are rich in nitrates and phosphates. Both of these chemicals are needed by plants for growth and so the farmer uses them on the land to make sure the next year's crop is a good one. One problem can be that some of these chemicals end up in the streams and rivers. Soil can be washed away, little by little, and the nutrients in the soil end up in the stream, river or lake. Another problem which can cause eutrophication is the disposal of sewage (human waste).

▲ *The effects of eutrophication can be seen in this river. Large growths of algae can be seen on the surface of the water.*

This material is often rich in bacteria and nutrients like nitrates and lots of it is pumped, untreated into rivers and the sea. As well as causing a health hazard the effect on the living plants and animals in the water can be dramatic.

WHAT IS THE EFFECT?

So what happens when these extra nutrients flow into water? The first effect is that the microscopic plants begin to multiply as the extra nutrients act like a fertiliser. The microscopic plants can grow very quickly, much faster than the larger water plants.

The effect of this growth is much more dramatic on still waters in lakes than in rivers because the nutrients accumulate in lakes and can't go anywhere. As the numbers of microscopic plants increase, the water becomes more and more cloudy. This blocks light from reaching the lower levels of the water. Many plants die as they can't produce food by photosynthesis because their light is blocked. As the plants die and decay they look and smell very unpleasant. They may release poisons into the water. Bacteria grow and use up the oxygen in the water, so fish and other water creatures die from lack of oxygen.

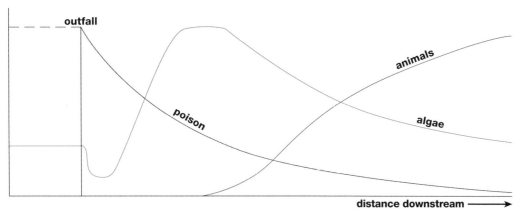

◄ *This graph shows the effect of sewage on the numbers of animals and algae in a river.*

THE DEAD SEA?

The sea can be affected by eutrophication. The Adriatic Sea off the coast of Italy was described by a marine biologist as being 'like a cappuccino of cosmic proportions' (cappuccino is Italian coffee with a thick froth on top). What he saw was a thick froth of rotting microscopic plants on the surface of the sea. Apart from anything else this was very bad for the tourist industry – people did not want to swim or sail in water which had this awful scum floating on the top!

Scientists are not absolutely sure why this eutrophication happened, but one possible cause could be the river Po which empties at least the following into the Adriatic each year:

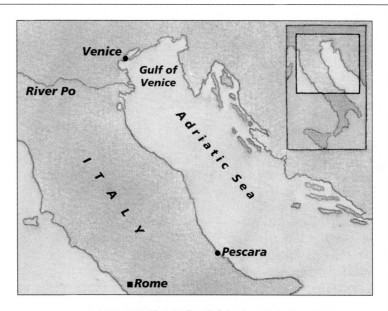

- ● *234 tonnes of arsenic*
- ● *65 tonnes of mercury*
- ● *20 000 tonnes of phosphate*
- ● *136 000 tonnes of nitrate*

Many scientists are convinced that a combination of hot summers and this nitrate had triggered a huge increase in *microscopic plants. Dead fish also started to appear near the floating scum, indicating a decrease in the oxygen levels. Just to give you an idea of how extensive the problem can be; in 1989 this floating raft of rotting microscopic plants stretched from Pescara (halfway down the Italian coast) right around the Gulf of Venice and along the coast of the Adriatic!*

USING ECHOES

Sound waves will reflect off an object; this means that the sound waves can be heard back at the place where they came from. Sound waves are compression waves that pass through the material that the sound is travelling in.

When you hear a telephone ring across a room the sound energy from the telephone is being carried to your ears by the sound waves passing across the room. It is important to realise that while the vibration of the sound is passed across the room by the air, the air itself does not travel across the room. A wave **transmits** energy but does not transmit matter.

WHAT IS AN ECHO?

The principle of the echo is simple. The wave leaves the source and travels to an object. It reflects off the object and a softer version of it is detected back at the source as it returns. A person standing 660 m from a tall cliff and making a loud noise will hear the echo 4 s after he or she makes the noise. This is because sound travels at about 330 ms^{-1} and it has to travel to the cliff and back again, a total distance of 1320 m.

▶ *Echoes are produced when sound waves bounce off a surface.*

> **D**ID YOU KNOW?
> Sonar takes its name from **so**und **n**avigation **a**nd **r**anging.

▶ *A system sends ultrasonic waves down into the water. The time taken for the echo to reach the system is measured.*

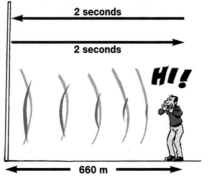

2 seconds

2 seconds

HI!

660 m

Echolocation

Echoes can be used to locate things. Imagine it is pitch dark and you want to know how far away you are from the cliff in the example above. If you make a loud noise and hear the echo after 1 s, then how far away from the cliff would you be? Sound travels at 330 m in 1 s. This must be the distance from you to the cliff and back again. So the cliff is 165 m away from you. We use the principle of **echolocation** in sonars, radar and ultrasound.

Sonar

Ships use echo sounding to find how deep the water is. **Sonar** is a similar device for finding underwater objects like submarines or shoals of fish.

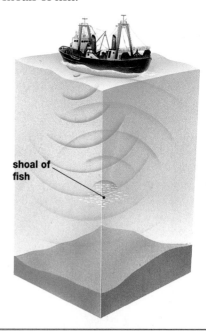

shoal of fish

> *Sonar was invented in 1915 by Professor Langevin in France. He developed the device to detect icebergs following the sinking of the passenger ship* Titanic *by an iceberg in 1912.*

DOPPLER EFFECT

The Doppler Effect is the name for the shift in pitch of a note when the source of the sound is moving away from or towards the observer. You notice this when a car with a siren or a motor bike goes past you very quickly. The note of the siren or engine goes from high to low as the vehicle moves towards you then away. This shift in pitch of the sound is actually a change in frequency. It is possible to measure the same type of frequency change when waves reflect off a moving object. Police use this method to tell how fast cars are moving along the road. Police speed checks with a 'radar gun' work out a motorist's speed by detecting the echo of an electro-magnetic wave. The gun sends out the wave and then detects the echo. A small computer system compares the echo with the original wave and calculates the speed of the car. The same idea can also be built into radar to tell how fast ships or aircraft are moving.

Radar

Radar is a similar idea where **electromagnetic waves**, like microwaves or radio waves, are used. A radar transmitter sends out pulses of radio-type waves from a rotating aerial. A solid metal object in the path of the beam would reflect some of the waves back to the aerial. The time gap between transmitting the pulse and receiving the reflection allows a computer to calculate how far away the object is. The screen output from the computer is often in the form of a map showing where all the surrounding objects are. This type of system is particularly useful for navigating ships and aircraft, especially in the fog or at night.

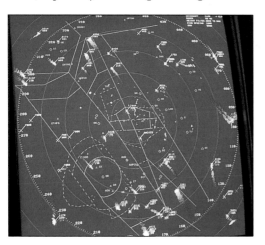

Animals use echolocation

With the development of radar and ultrasound we appear to be quite advanced. The humbling thing to remember is that even our best radar has a long way to go to match the echolocation used by bats, dolphins and some birds. These animals have evolved with their own biological inbuilt 'radar' systems. They work on the basis of ultrasound-type pulses that are sent out and then detected by the animal. Bats are able to use their 'radar' to fly at high speed in the dark to avoid objects that are in the way and catch flying insects.

◄ Air traffic control systems use radar. The control tower sends out radio waves which are reflected from aircraft. The time taken for the signal to return is used to calculate the distance to the aircraft and this information is shown on the screen.

▲ Dolphins navigate using echolocation. They make high-pitched noises which bounce off objects in the form of echoes.

DID YOU KNOW?

The word radar comes from **ra**dio **d**irection **a**nd **r**anging.

Ultrasound

Echoes are also important in medicine. Ultrasound is pressure waves, like sound waves, with a frequency higher than 20 000 Hz so that it is not audible to humans. These ultrasound waves will pass through the human body and the faint echoes can be detected and processed by a computer to give an image of the soft tissue inside without causing any damage. This is very useful for studying unborn babies to make sure that all is well. The proper name for ultrasound examination is ultrasound scanning.

■ *For more about ultrasound see p17.*

HEARING SOUND

What's happening

How do you know what is going on around you? You can tell because you see, smell, taste, hear and touch. These are your senses.

SIGHT

We rely on our eyes a tremendous amount, usually more than any other sense. Human eyes are very good at seeing details and seeing colours, but the eyes of some animals can see some things that humans can't.

An insect eye is very different from a human eye. It has many lenses instead of only one, and the picture an insect sees is probably very different from the picture we see. For example, some flowers have special markings that act as guidelines, helping insects to find the nectar in the centre of the flower. But although insects follow the guidelines easily, many of the markings are invisible to humans.

Hawks and other birds of prey have amazingly powerful eyesight. They can see a tiny vole moving through grass while they are hovering far above the ground. Their

▲ *This geranium has nectar guides on its petals used by bees.*

distance vision is far better than ours. Owls have still more spectacular powers of sight. Their huge eyes can detect small movements, even in darkness. They are much more sensitive in low-light conditions than our eyes.

■ **For more about the eye see pp102–3.**

SMELL AND TASTE

Some animals have very bad eyesight or no eyesight at all! Many insects like moths are active at night when their eyesight is of little use. This suggests that moths have some other method of finding their way about. The most important part of an insect's senses are its antennae. These delicate structures contain cells which are sensitive to different chemicals.

This is similar to smell and taste in humans. In moths, as with many other animals, including humans, the senses of smell and taste are closely linked. But the insect sense of smell/taste is much more sensitive than ours.

Some male moths can detect the presence of a female moth without seeing her and over long distances – as much as 1.6 km. The female moth produces a chemical called **pheromone** *and this chemical can be detected by the male moth, using its antennae. Farmers have used this sensitivity to attract some insects away from crops by laying down false pheromone trails! Insects that live in large groups, like ants, termites and bees, use pheromones to pass messages through the colony.*

◀ ***This insect antennae is magnified and shows the divisions that catch molecules of pheromone from females.***

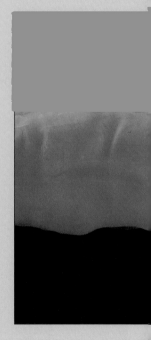

OUT there?

HEARING

Hearing is very important for humans, but the most astonishing example of an animal with a highly developed sense of hearing is the bat. Fruit bats have good vision, but the smaller insect-eating bats depend on echolocation to find their way around. These bats have very small eyes of little use for flying at night and their eyes are certainly no good for following a moth and catching it in mid-flight.

Bats catch moths by a method that works rather like **radar**. The British invented radar during the Second World War. They used radio waves to detect enemy aircraft long before they came in sight, either by night or by day. Bats have used a kind of radar, using sound waves instead of radio, for millions of years, and their system works far better than radar does. Bats produce and can detect sounds that are far too high for us to hear.

These high sounds bounce back or echo from anything that gets in their way.

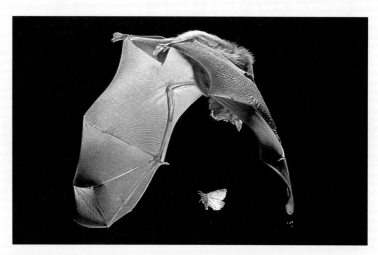

The bat's large ears collect some of the echoes, and the animal can understand what they mean. For example, it can tell the difference between a flying insect and other animals; if it is chasing a moth it can even judge the position of the moth and its speed.

■ *For more about echoes and radar see pp60–61.*

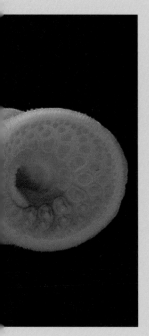

Insects are sensitive to a lot of other chemicals. Some butterflies recognise plants not by their flower colours but by the smell of their leaves or flowers. Different plants produce different chemicals and these may attract different insects.

Fish have a powerful sense of smell, too. The lamprey is a **parasitic** fish which sucks the blood of other fish. A lamprey will get excited if just a little water from the tank containing another fish is added to its own tank. It can 'detect' the other fish even in these very small quantities. Sharks also have a good sense of smell – they are able to detect blood in the water from an injured animal several kilometres away.

◄ *This shows the mouth of a lamprey. It attaches to the fish and sucks out the fish's body fluids.*

TOUCH

Fish rely heavily on their sense of touch, or rather on the messages they get from vibrations in the water, to understand what is happening around them. The most famous example of this is the shark, which can recognise the difference between the movements of an animal swimming normally and those of an animal that is hurt or distressed in some way, which might be easier to catch.

Darwin's

*In 1831, a ship called the **Beagle** set out from Britain on an expedition to survey the coasts of South America and the currents of the Pacific Ocean. A young naturalist called Charles Darwin (1809–82) was invited to go on this expedition. His job was to examine and collect any animals and plants which were interesting or unusual. The expedition lasted for five years.*

At the time the *Beagle* sailed, many scientists thought that the Earth had never changed from the moment it had formed. Others thought that the Earth was changing gradually, and that over millions of years it had changed greatly. One of these scientists, Adam Sedgewick, had taught Darwin when he was a student. At that time, most people thought that all the different animals and plants on Earth had been created simultaneously, and had never changed since then.

Darwin's observations

Darwin saw lots of interesting things during the voyage, for example he noticed that on the top of a mountain in South America there were many fossilised sea shells!

He also noticed interesting things on islands. Most scientists expected all animals and plants on islands to be similar, because they believed that such animals and plants had been created specifically to live on islands. But Darwin noticed that the animals and plants on the Cape Verde Islands (look for these islands on the map) were more like those from the mainland of Africa, while animals and plants on the Galapagos Islands were rather like those of South America. When he compared the animals and plants of the two groups of islands, however, they were not alike.

The most interesting thing of all was that although many of the Galapagos Islands were similar, each little island had its own variety of animals. The animals from each island were distinctly different from those of the others.

■ *For more about evolution see pp66–7.*

NORTH ATLANTIC OCEAN

Cape Verde Islands

Galapagos Islands

SOUTH AMERICA

SOUTH ATLANTIC OCEAN

▶ *Darwin's route.*

Cape Horn

hard nuts and large seeds

small seeds

voyage

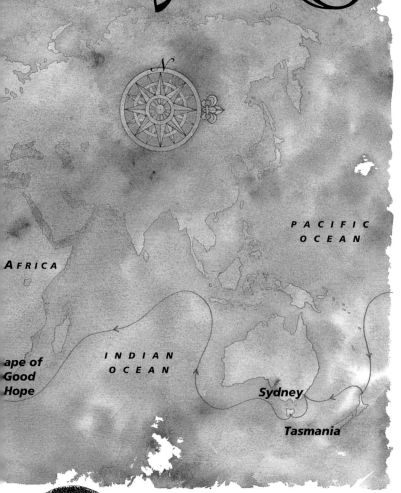

AFRICA

ape of
Good
Hope

INDIAN
OCEAN

PACIFIC
OCEAN

Sydney

Tasmania

insects

grubs

◀ *Darwin observed
many species of finch
on the Galapagos
Islands. Each was
adapted to eat a
different type of food.
You can see this from
the birds' different-
shaped beaks.*

ADAM SEDGEWICK AND CHARLES LYELL

*I*n the 19th
century, geology
(the study of
the Earth), was a
particularly exciting
branch of science to
be involved with. Two
famous British
geologists were Charles
Lyell (1797–1875) and Adam
Sedgewick (1785–1873).

**Adam
Sedgewick**

Charles Lyell, in an
important book called Principles of
Geology, *said that changes in the Earth
had mainly taken place gradually and
over long periods of time. Adam Sedgewick
was one of Charles Darwin's teachers at
Cambridge University. During one of his
geological trips with Sedgewick, Darwin
wrote, 'Nothing before had ever made me
realise . . . that science
consists in grouping facts
so that general laws or
conclusions may be
drawn from them.'
His study of
geology and
geological ideas
may well have
laid the
foundations for
Darwin's
revolutionary theory
of* **evolution by
natural selection.**

Charles Lyell

LIFE GOES ON

Darwin's theory of evolution

▲ *Charles Darwin (1809–1882)*

When Darwin returned home from the voyage he thought for a long time about what he had seen. He began to think that animals and plants might change over periods of time.

If, he argued, the Earth can change so dramatically that sea shells that once must have been on the sea bed are now on top of a mountain, then perhaps animals and plants can change too.

Darwin suggested several ideas to explain his observations:

● Animals and plants can change over many generations, over long periods of time;
● Different kinds of bee, such as the honey bee and the bumble bee, are quite similar. Originally, there may have been only one type of bee. Over a very long period of time this bee has **evolved** into the many different types of bee that we now see. Other similar groups, such as cats, lions and leopards, or the various kinds of bean plant, may have evolved from a single type of animal or plant in the same way;
● Animals and plants on islands originally came from the mainland. They gradually became isolated and, over long periods of time, some developed certain differences from the mainland animals and plants.

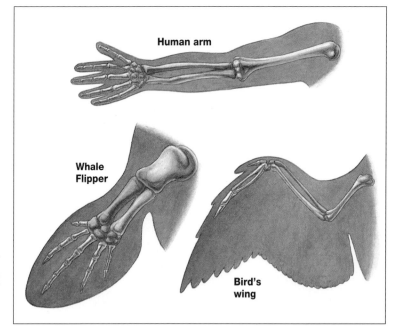

▲ *The forelimbs of a human, a bird and a whale have similar features. Each has a different function, but the similarity in the pattern of bones gives us evidence of evolution from a common source.*

Natural selection

Darwin's theory of evolution is based on these observations and deductions:

- Many species of animals and plants breed rapidly but, even so, population sizes remain more-or-less constant;
- Some animals are better fitted to survive in an environment (survival of the fittest) than others.

The individuals of a species always vary, for example some can run faster, some have better camouflage. The individuals that are best adapted for an environment may survive best and have the most offspring. The offspring tend to resemble their parents and some of the useful features are passed on to the next generation. So the species may become successful in these environmental conditions. But conditions are not the same everywhere, so a variation that is useful in one area may not be useful in another. A species can, therefore, evolve differently in different places and give rise to individuals which are adapted in different ways in different environments. This is **natural selection**.

It is often those animals or plants which are best adapted which don't survive long term. When conditions change again, the most highly adapted find it difficult to re-adapt to fit the new conditions!

Darwin called the gradual change of animals and plants over long periods of time **evolution**. His ideas are extremely important in science, because they help us to understand how life on Earth had changed and is changing.

TAKING A HAND IN EVOLUTION

People produce evolution artificially by breeding animals or plants in particular ways. Think of all the different breeds of dog there are. Once, it is thought, all dogs looked like the wolf. Humans have domesticated the dog and bred hunting dogs, guard dogs, sheep dogs, miniature dogs, and so on. All came originally from an animal like the wolf!

'The origin of species'

At first, Darwin was too frightened of criticism to write about his ideas, but in 1859 he put them into a book called *On the origin of species by means of natural selection*. The book caused a sensation when it was published and sold out on the first day. Everyone was discussing it, and Darwin became famous. But even today, some people still find it hard to accept Darwin's idea of evolution.

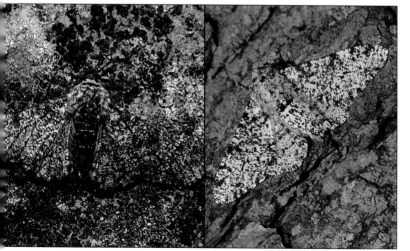

◄ *Peppered moths can come in two forms, dark and light. At one time, nearly all peppered moths were light. Only a few were dark and these could easily be seen by predators (birds) against a tree-trunk. However, during the 1800s, smoke from factories blackened tree-trunks. At this time the light moths became easier to spot, while the dark moths were camouflaged. So more of the white moths were eaten and their numbers declined. The dark moths flourished – an example of natural selection!*

WHAT MENDEL DID

A farmer had two pregnant cows. When their calves were born, one was strong and healthy but the other was small and weak. The farmer knew that the strong calf had been fathered by an old bull belonging to a friend of hers, and the little weak one by the local prize bull.

The owner of the prize bull did not believe her. He demanded his stud fee in full! He told everyone in the village that it was obvious that this splendid animal could produce only healthy calves. It couldn't possibly father a weakling, you could tell just by looking at it.

The farmers argued until, eventually, they decided to clear up the argument once and for all. Samples of blood were taken from all the animals. When they were tested it was discovered that the weak calf probably was the offspring of the prize bull, and the healthy calf probably was the offspring of the old bull.

> **G**regor Mendel (1822–84) was an Austrian monk and amateur botanist. Through his experiments on pea plants he noticed patterns from one generation to the next, now known as Mendel's laws of heredity.
> Heredity is the transfer of characteristics from one generation to the next. In humans examples of inherited characteristics are the colour of your eyes and your blood group.

Genetics

The farmer who owned the prize bull had made certain assumptions. He had assumed that 'like begets like'. That is, he believed that because the prize bull was big and healthy, all his offspring would be big and healthy, too – but

▼ **Which bull fathered which calf?**

that doesn't always happen. He had also assumed that the male (that is, the bull) is the main factor in deciding what the offspring is like – but that isn't always true, either.

The branch of science called **genetics**, studies how characteristics are passed on from parents to offspring.

Gregor Mendel

By making observations of a family tree we can see that characteristics are passed on from one generation to the next.

The first person to do experiments on how characteristics are passed on was a monk called Gregor Mendel. Mendel did his experiments in the late 19th century.

What Mendel did was to experiment carefully, and record family trees and their characteristics exactly. He couldn't use humans for his experiments: humans take too long to reproduce – and, besides, we can't control who has children or how many they have! So he used plants

RUNNING IN FAMILIES

Before Mendel's experiments, many doctors and surgeons knew that some physical features were passed on in families. One famous example was the royal family of Habsburg, which ruled over Austria and Hungary. Certain members of this family had a curiously shaped lower lip, which stuck right out; it even became known as the Habsburg lip. But not every member of the family had this. Somehow the characteristic lip had been passed on from one to another, but at the time no-one understood how this happened.

The Holy Roman Emperor Charles V looks to have had a Habsburg lip.

instead. Plants can be crossed just like animals, and in many ways plants are better to use because you get a lot more offspring from them. Mendel studied the pea plants that were growing in the garden of the monastery where he lived.

MENDEL'S PEA PLANT EXPERIMENTS

Pea plants have different characteristics such as:

- some pea plants produce seeds which are wrinkled and some produce seeds which are round
- some pea plants produce green seeds, some produce yellow seeds
- some pea plants have long stems and are tall (about 2 m), others have short stems and are dwarf (about 1 m)

Mendel used the last characteristic for his experiments. He crossed a tall pea plant with a dwarf pea plant, then he collected all the seeds that were produced and grew them all. He found that *all* these seeds grew into tall pea plants. The dwarfness seemed to have disappeared. But when he crossed these new plants with one another something

strange happened. The dwarfness reappeared in some of the offspring (see the diagram below).

Mendel found this pattern with many of the other characteristics of pea plants which he studied. He could then predict what would happen when two pea plants were crossed. The basic rules which Mendel discovered in pea plants can be used in many other plants, and in animals, too.

Strangely enough, nobody thought Mendel's work was very important at the time. It was only after many years that other scientists realised the importance of his experiments.

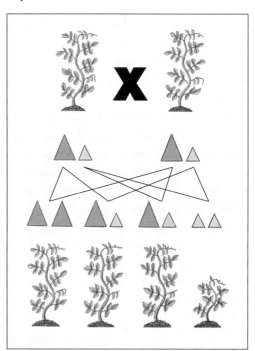

Genetics today

Genetics is one of the most important of all the sciences. Breeding programmes to produce healthy, disease-resistant plants and animals depend upon understanding how characteristics are passed on from one generation to the next. Some diseases in humans like **haemophilia** and **cystic fibrosis** are inherited, and genetics has helped us understand how they are passed on. Drugs like **insulin** can now be manufactured in large quantities using bacteria because we have come to understand bacterial genetics.

■ *For more about inherited diseases see p71.*

FAMILIES *that are* DIFFERENT

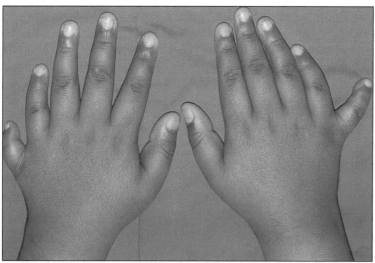

▲ *This person has a variation of an extra finger on each hand.*

Human beings and all other living things show **variations**. We are so used to most of these human variations that we take them for granted. People with blue or brown eyes are considered to be perfectly 'normal', but some variations occur less often and catch our attention. For example, six-fingered dwarfism, although rare in most parts of the world, frequently occurs in some families in Lancaster County, Pennsylvania, in the United States.

One of the most interesting things about variations is the way some of them run in families. They are passed down from generation to generation and are called **genetic variations**. When unusual variations occur in families that have some famous members, scientists have a good chance of studying how they are inherited. The detail of these families, such as who each member married and how many children they had, can often be found out easily.

■ *For more about genetics see p69.*

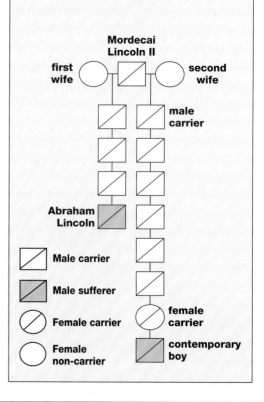

THE LINCOLN FAMILY GENES

*The sixteenth President of the United States, Abraham Lincoln (1809–65), had extremely long legs and thumbs of different sizes. The condition is caused by a particular **gene**, but it shows up in families only from time to time. Some of the members of the family carry the gene but do not show its effects. You can see how this condition occurs in part of the Lincoln family tree.*

Mordecai Lincoln II

first wife · second wife

male carrier

Abraham Lincoln

☒ Male carrier
▨ Male sufferer
⊘ Female carrier
◯ Female non-carrier

female carrier

contemporary boy

Hereditary diseases

Sometimes genetic variations are harmful to the people who possess them and we call them diseases. They are not caught by coming into contact with disease-causing microorganisms like catching 'flu or measles. **Genetic diseases** happen because particular forms of genes are passed down in the families of the sufferers. Unfortunately, most genetic or **hereditary** diseases like this have no cure as yet. Many people with hereditary diseases do not 'look' different from other people and their disease has to be diagnosed by a doctor.

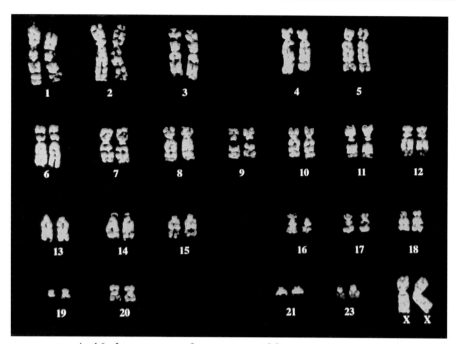

▲ 46 chromosomes from a normal human female. This is the total number of chromosomes found in cells of the female human body.

CYSTIC FIBROSIS

One of the most common genetic diseases in Britain is called **cystic fibrosis**. It affects about one child in 2000 in Britain. These children have repeated lung infections and digestive problems, and may have to spend a great deal of their lives in hospital.

The position on the chromosome of the gene responsible for cystic fibrosis has recently been identified. It was found at a particular point on chromosome seven after many years of scientific research in Britain, Canada and the United States.

This discovery is very important because it makes it possible to test parents who may be carriers of cystic fibrosis to see if they are carrying the gene. So, although a cure for the disease may be a way off yet, a high-risk couple can be counselled about any diffi cult decisions they may have to make.

SICKLE CELL ANAEMIA

The photograph on the right shows what can happen to the red blood cells of people who have the hereditary disease called **sickle cell anaemia**. Not enough oxygen can be carried by the blood, as the red blood cells are defective, and the sufferer may get fevers and severe pains. The disease is very rare in Britain and northern Europe but it is more common in America, Africa, Arabia, India and parts of southern Europe. The reasons for this odd pattern

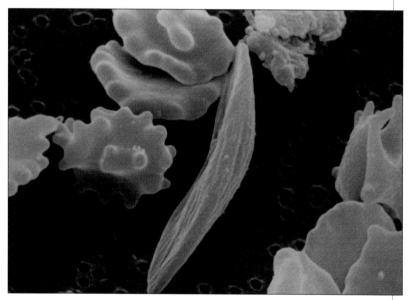

▲ The central blood cell is deformed into the sickle shape. The surrounding cells are normal red cells.

are complicated. Other hereditary diseases also occur more frequently in some populations than in others. In Finland, for example, cystic fibrosis is ten times more rare than in most other countries.

■ *For more about diseases see pp144–155.*

Test-tu

Daily

And her

THE

L

> *Unfortunately some couples who want to have a baby are unable to do so. In the United Kingdom infertility affects about a million couples. The partners may produce perfectly normal sperm and eggs in the right numbers for fertilisation, but it just doesn't happen.*

In vitro *fertilisation*

One way scientists have found of solving this problem is by fertilising the woman's eggs with her partner's own sperm outside the woman's body. This is called *in vitro* **fertilisation** (IVF). *In vitro* comes from the Latin phrase meaning 'in glass' and is so called because fertilisation happens in a sterile glass Petri dish. It's not quite as easy as it sounds because sperm and eggs have to be carefully prepared and collected.

Sperm are more easily collected than eggs: the man collects his own **semen** (the fluid containing sperm) in a container. The woman is treated for several days with drugs that make her prepare several eggs in each ovary for release. Usually only one egg is released each month. The doctor is able to check how many eggs are developing in the ovaries by taking an ultrasound scan picture of the woman's abdomen. In the scan, the doctor can see the fluid-filled cavities, called **follicles**, in which the eggs develop.

The next stage is to remove the eggs from the ovaries just before they would normally be released. This is done either by a small operation or by dislodging the eggs using ultrasound which does not require a general anaesthetic.

■ *For more about ultrasound scans see p17.*

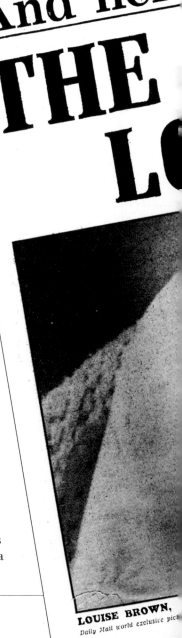

▶ *Louise Brown was the first test-tube baby born, in 1978.*

If an operation is involved the surgeon uses a special instrument called a **laparoscope**, which is placed into the abdomen through a small hole. This lets the surgeon look into the abdomen to find the ovaries.

The surgeon then inserts a fine needle into each follicle of the ovaries and the eggs are sucked out into a small jar.

LOUISE BROWN,
Daily Mail world exclusive pic

be babies

Mail 8p

she is...

LOVELY LOUISE

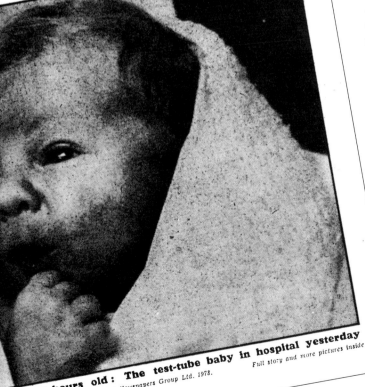

ed at 18 hours old: **The test-tube baby in hospital yesterday**

Full story and more pictures inside

ROSS. World Copyright Associated Newspapers Group Ltd. 1978.

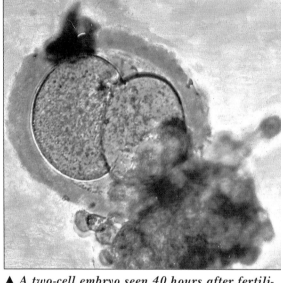

▲ *A two-cell embryo seen 40 hours after fertilisation. The cells are shown in red. Each cell will continue to divide to form a human composed of millions of cells. (Magnification ✕ 1700).*

PRODUCING THE EMBRYO

The sperm and eggs are kept at 37 ˚C (body temperature) in the laboratory, mixed together, and checked to see if fertilisation has taken place. One or two days later if the embryos are developing properly they are placed in the woman's womb using a thin plastic tube. This does not require anaesthetic.

Usually the doctor places between three and seven healthy embryos in the womb, trying to ensure that one will become attached to the wall and the woman will become pregnant. On average about 30 per cent of women who receive this treatment do become pregnant. Since Louise Brown was born in 1978, many thousands of babies have been conceived in this way in many different parts of the world.

Test-tu

Gift

More recently a slightly different method has been developed called **g**amete **i**ntrafallopian **t**ransfer (GIFT). Sperm and eggs are collected in the same way as for IVF. Then eggs and sperm are sucked into a thin plastic tube and injected directly into the **fallopian tube** (oviduct). The surgeon is able to see to do this by using the laparoscope. Fertilisation takes place in the fallopian tube.

This natural environment for fertilisation is a major advantage and the success rate is double that of IVF. GIFT is only possible for women with undamaged fallopian tubes. Many hospitals in the United Kingdom already offer both IVF and GIFT treatment and, it is likely that many more will be able to do so in the future.

▶ *The development of techniques such as IVF and GIFT has helped lots of couples but has resulted in some controversial treatments of older women.*

Triplets for a sterile mum, 58

Miracle birth a world first

A 58-YEAR-OLD set a world record by giving birth to triplets... And she was completely STERILE.

Elide Accili, from Pescara, on the east coast of Italy, went to a clinic in Naples eight months ago.

She was fertilised with eggs given by an unknown female donor.

These were impregnated into her uterus after her husband Antonino gave his sperm.

The triplets – two boys and a girl – were born by caesarean

By PAUL HOUSE

operation on Saturday afternoon.

The mother and her babies are all said to be doing well.

Elide had gone through her menopause and was completely sterile.

But professor Raffaele Magli – who runs the clinic – used

the in-vitro techniqu to fertilise the eggs a laboratory and the impregnate her.

The operation h been a total succ and the family, who smallholders, are to be absolut delighted.

The Guinness of Records ha account of a st woman giving bi triplets in this w

be babies

Is it ethical?

Such techniques have produced a number of problems. These are not medical but **ethical** problems; that means problems of whether or not we should use these treatments.

For example:

POINT	Many people think that helping people to have babies is a good thing.
QUESTION	*But, should we help a woman to have a baby if she is 62 years of age?*
POINT	It seems sensible to fertilise ten eggs rather than just one, as this gives the woman a better chance of a successful pregnancy if more fertilised eggs are placed inside her womb.
QUESTION	*But, what should we do with the fertile eggs which are not put inside the womb? Should one woman's egg be put into the womb of a different woman? Should unused fertile eggs be studied by scientists to find out more about how fertile eggs develop?*
POINT	As the test-tube baby techniques get better, more and more couples can be helped.
QUESTION	*But, the money could be spent on treatments which save lives, like kidney transplants or cancer research.*

There may be no clear-cut answers to questions such as these, but decisions are being made as the practice of test-tube babies becomes more common.

TEST TUBE MUM AT 62

FURY AS DOCTORS BREED 'ORPHANS'

A TEST-TUBE mother is to become the world's oldest woman ever to give birth — at 62.

She has become pregnant with the help of donor eggs and artificial insemination after 39 years of childless marriage.

The pregnancy has renewed worldwide controversy over test-tube babies.

Dr Mike MacNamee, science director at the pioneering Bourn Hall Clinic in Cambridgeshire, said last night: "It is ethically unacceptable to create orphans. Both parents could be infirm or even dead before the unborn child reaches its teens. This is generation-hopping. It

by NICKI POPE and GRAHAM BROUGH

is clearly wrong to produce a child in women beyond their reproductive years."

Concetta di Tessa pleaded with doctors in Naples, Italy, to help her become pregnant to save her marriage.

The donor eggs were fertilised by her husband, a 56-year-old greengrocer. Her child will be born in August.

She went through the menopause nearly 14 years ago, before the first test-tube baby was born in Britain in 1978.

"We have wanted a child for almost 40 years and never had one," she said yesterday. "Now at last I can be a mother with my own child. We are very, very happy.

WHAT makes

In 1827 a Scottish scientist called Robert Brown was looking through a microscope at some pollen grains suspended in water. He noticed something unusual – the pollen grains were moving about!

Pollen is produced by many plants. Each species of plant produces its own type of pollen: pollen from roses is quite different from grass pollen. The pollen grains that Robert Brown was looking at were tiny.

Like all good scientists Brown tried to explain his observation. He had seen tiny pollen grains jiggling about in a random way when they were suspended in water. Because the pollen came from a plant which was a living thing, Brown suggested that 'vitality is retained . . . long after the plant's death'. He meant that the pollen was a living thing like the plant it had come from, and that it continued to live and move after the plant had died.

Moving particles

Some time later Brown focussed his microscope on some water trapped in a piece of transparent rock called **quartz**. The water had been trapped when the rock was formed, millions of years ago. Brown saw tiny particles of dust suspended in the water drop. The dust particles were moving in a similar way to the pollen grains he had seen before. Brown decided that the water in the rock could not contain any living material, because it had been sealed in for millions of years. The explanation he had

used for the pollen could not be applied to the dust. Rather than try to find a way of fitting his old theory to his new results, Brown concluded (quite correctly) that he had been wrong. The movement was nothing to do with living things at all.

Brownian motion

At the time, other scientists were not very interested in Brown's observations. They suggested the motion was caused by tiny convection currents in the liquid (see below).

▶ *If one part of a fluid is hotter than another part the hot part moves upwards, as it cools it drops down again. This happens because the hot fluid is less dense than the cool fluid.*

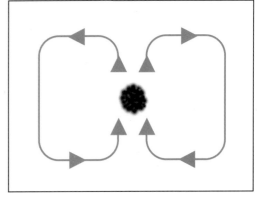

But in a convection current all the particles are seen to move in roughly the same direction. If you observe **Brownian motion** (as it has come to be known) you will see that all the particles move independently of each other.

▼ *An easy method of observing Brownian motion is to look through a microscope at smoke particles suspended in air.*

*R**obert Brown (1773–1858) was a Scottish botanist and physicist. He studied the random motion of pollen grains in water in 1827. This effect is known as Brownian motion and was seen as evidence of the existence of atoms and molecules.*

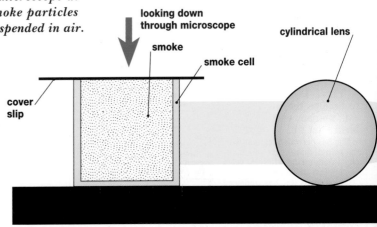

looking down through microscope

smoke

smoke cell

cylindrical lens

cover slip

nem M⬤VE?

By 1905 the following things were known about Brownian motion:

- the movement was random
- it did not stop
- although different bits of dust showed the same sort of motion there was no connection between them
- the movement was more agitated at higher temperatures
- the larger the particle, the slower its Brownian motion.

People began to suspect that the Brownian motion was caused by *the fluid in which the bits of matter were suspended*. Perhaps, they thought, the fluid was made up of very tiny *invisible* particles that were knocking the bits of pollen and dust about.

Einstein

The now-famous physicist Albert Einstein worked out an equation that could be used to test the above explanation of Brownian motion. Einstein's equation was also used to make the first accurate estimate of the mass of an atom.

■ *For more about atoms see pp78–81.*

▼ *The air molecules bombard the smoke particle, causing it to move.*

A lbert Einstein (1879–1955) was a physicist who was born in Ulm, Germany. He became a Swiss citizen in 1901 and left Germany for the United States in 1933. He is most famous for developing the theory of relativity. His theories are the basis for many of our ideas about the history and structure of the Universe!

Today

We take it for granted today that matter is made up of tiny invisible particles called atoms. In gases and liquids these particles are all on the move. A gas is a collection of such particles flying about very rapidly, rebounding off each other and any other objects they meet. In a liquid the tiny particles are closer to each other but they still move about, knocking against each other and against other objects.

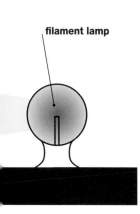

filament lamp

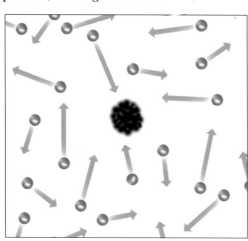

The Story

In around 400 BC a Greek philosopher named Democritus asked the question: Is there a point beyond which it is impossible to break up a piece of material into smaller pieces? He came to the conclusion that such a point did exist. He imagined that all materials were made up of extremely small, hard spheres which were impossible to break up. Democritus called these spheres atoms, from the Greek word 'atomos', meaning indivisible (cannot be divided up). Just by thinking, Democritus had made a picture in his mind (a **model**) of atoms as tiny hard spheres, a bit like snooker balls. More than 2000 years later, scientists still accepted Democritus' model until, in the 1890s, new experimental results began to throw doubt on this idea of **atomic structure**.

1879 AD. William Crookes was investigating the effect of very high electrical voltages on samples of gases. These experiments were carried out in glass tubes, now known as **Crookes' tubes**. In the experiments Crookes found that rays were given off, and that they carried a negative electric charge.

1895 A German scientist called Wilhelm Röntgen was also experimenting with atoms. He noticed that photographic plates which had been left near a Crookes' tube by accident were affected by the rays that came from the tube. These rays were similar in some ways to light, but were different because they could also penetrate solids. Röntgen called the unknown rays X-rays. He found that X-rays were produced when fast-moving rays hit a metal target.

■ *For more about X-rays see p16.*

1896 Henri Becquerel, professor of physics at the University of Paris, showed that substances containing uranium also produced rays that were like these X-rays.

1897 The English scientist John Joseph Thomson, then professor of physics at the University of Cambridge, was studying the nature of the rays given off in Crookes' experiments. He carried out experiments using several

▲ *Crookes' tubes.*

▼ *Plum-pudding model of the atom. The negative electrons were thought to be embedded in the positive solid sphere of the atom.*

different substances, and found that all of them gave off the same kind of rays. He concluded that they were not rays at all but streams of minute particles of matter. His work showed that the particles were much lighter than any atom.

Thomson called the negatively charged particles electrons. He suggested that the electrons had been pulled off the gas atoms by the effect of the high voltage. Since he knew that an atom as a whole had no charge, he came to believe that atoms were solid spheres of positive charge with electrons embedded in them, the charge from the electrons would balance the positive charge. To describe the invisible atoms in terms of a familiar object, this new model was likened to a plum-pudding (Christmas pudding), the electrons being the plums.

of the AT⊙M

1898 Marie and Pierre Curie extracted two new elements from **pitchblende**, the raw materials from which uranium was obtained. The two new elements were far more active than uranium at producing rays. These 'radioactive' elements were named **polonium** and **radium**. Marie Curie was the first person to use the word **radiation** to describe the rays given off by the elements she was experimenting with. Marie and Pierre's work gave other scientists powerful tools for further experimentation. The new element, polonium gave off three types of radiation. These were named from the first three letters of the Greek alphabet α, β and ψ. Knowledge of these types of radiation formed the next stage in understanding the structure of atoms.

▲ *Ernest Rutherford (1871–1937) was awarded the Nobel Prize for Chemistry in 1908.*

1911 Ernest Rutherford's experiment of 'feeling' atoms using α particles was carried out at Manchester by two of his assistants, Ernest Marsden and Hans Geiger. A very thin sheet of gold foil was bombarded with α particles. The polonium used to produce the α particles was a present from Marie Curie. As expected, many of the α particles passed straight through the foil. However, some made large changes in direction.

▼ *Most of the α particles went through the gold foil (A) but some changed direction slightly (B) and a few bounced back (C).*

M arie Curie (1867–1934) was a Polish physicist. In 1891 she emigrated to Paris and studied at Sorbonne University. There, she met Pierre Curie and they married in 1895. They researched radioactivity and shared the Nobel Prize for Physics in 1903 with Henri Becquerel (the discoverer of radioactivity). In 1911 Marie was awarded the Nobel Prize for Chemistry. She died from cancer, probably brought on from working so long with radioactive materials without protection.

◄ *Marie Curie working in her laboratory. She named the radioactive element polonium after her homeland, Poland.*

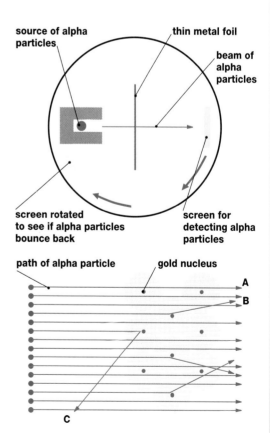

source of alpha particles

thin metal foil

beam of alpha particles

screen rotated to see if alpha particles bounce back

screen for detecting alpha particles

path of alpha particle

gold nucleus

A
B

C

The Story

Rutherford could only explain these observations by making the assumption that the atoms of gold consisted mostly of empty space, with very tiny but heavy central cores which were positively charged. He used the word **nucleus** to describe the core of the atom. His picture of the atom was very different from Thomson's plum-pudding model.

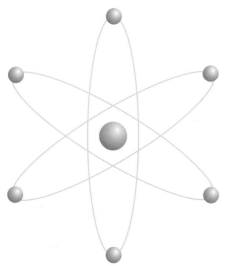

▲ *Rutherford's work had resulted in a new model of the atom as spheres of fast-moving electrons orbiting round a very small positively charged nucleus.*

Protons

Rutherford then went on to try to find out what the nucleus of an atom is actually like. He guessed that since hydrogen was the simplest of all atoms it would have the simplest atomic structure. He thought it was possible that all atoms were in some way built up from hydrogen atoms. In 1919, after many years of careful experimentation, he showed that hydrogen nuclei could be knocked out of the nuclei of atoms.

The hydrogen nucleus was given the name **proton**, and Rutherford concluded that the nuclei of all atoms were built up of protons. He found a relationship between the number of protons in the nucleus of an atom and the **atomic number** of the atom. (Atomic numbers at that time were simply the numbers given to the elements set out in order of relative **atomic mass**, as in Mendeleev's Periodic Table.) He found that the atomic number was the same as the number of protons in the nucleus of the atom. But Rutherford could not find a relationship between the relative atomic mass of an atom and the number of protons in its nucleus.

■ *For more about atoms and the Periodic Table see pp96–7.*

proton

neutron

▶ *A model of the atom as we know it today. This represents an atom of potassium with a central nucleus surrounded by 'shells' of electrons. Another model is to imagine the electrons like planets orbiting the sun (the nucleus).*

of the ATOM

Neutrons

electron

In 1920 Rutherford imagined that in the nucleus of an atom, as well as protons, there could be another kind of particle. This would be as heavy as the proton but did not have a charge. He named this 'imaginary' particle the **neutron**. To prove his theory was extremely difficult, since all the known methods used to show the presence of particles only worked for charged particles. Rutherford compared the neutron to the 'invisible man' in order to suggest how its presence would be proved. He said, 'How could you find the invisible man in Piccadilly Circus (a busy area of London)? You couldn't see him but you'd know he was there by the reactions of the people he pushed aside.' Rutherford began work to find this particle at about the same time that he started a new job as professor of physics in charge of the Cavendish Laboratory at the University of Cambridge. There he was leading a large team of scientists. He set them searching for the neutron. James Chadwick was a member of this team.

The atom as we know it today

James Chadwick eventually proved that the neutron existed. This happened 12 years after Rutherford had predicted that it was present. His discovery completed the planetary model of the atom, now so familiar to students of science in schools. The story did not stop there. More recently scientists have suggested that neutrons and protons are themselves made of even smaller particles.

◄ *James Chadwick discovered the neutron using this apparatus.*

CHEMICAL REACTIONS *and* ENERGY

When chemical reactions take place there is an energy change. Sometimes the energy change is large and can be measured easily, sometimes the energy change is small and difficult to measure.

A change in temperature is an easy way of measuring energy changes. Temperature may decrease or increase during a chemical reaction. Changes in temperature are caused because heat energy is either released or taken in during the reaction. Some reactions release heat energy and cause a temperature rise. These are called **exothermic** reactions. Other reactions absorb heat energy from the surroundings and cause a temperature drop. These are called **endothermic** reactions.

Below are some reactions which release energy as heat:

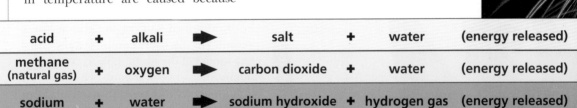

acid	+	alkali	➡	salt	+	water	(energy released)
methane (natural gas)	+	oxygen	➡	carbon dioxide	+	water	(energy released)
sodium	+	water	➡	sodium hydroxide	+	hydrogen gas	(energy released)

▶ *Sometimes the energy change can be seen. In some chemical reactions light energy is also released, for example when magnesium ribbon burns. This reaction releases lots of light energy as well as heat energy.*

▲ *Each chemical used to produce the colour in fireworks emits light of a specific colour, e.g. magnesium (white), sodium compounds (yellow), copper compounds (blue).*

Exothermic reactions in and out of control

Many exothermic reactions are very important, especially the burning of fuels. A fuel is a substance that reacts to produce heat. Most common fuels react with oxygen and release energy as heat. So coal, oil, gases of various types and wood are all common fuels. The fuels that we burn in our homes are burned in a controlled way. The heat energy is released gradually. In a gas burner, like the Bunsen burner, the flow of gas is controlled and mixed with oxygen (from the air) a little at a time. The release of heat is gradual and controlled, but there are dangers. If there is a gas leak, even a small one, and gas gradually accumulates inside a house, a tiny spark (from a light switch) may be enough to cause a chemical reaction which involves all the escaped gas. If this happens then all the heat energy is released at once, in a fraction of a second!

This is an uncontrolled chemical reaction which we call an explosion. For this reason gas appliances must be well ventilated so that any leaking gas can escape. This is a problem with gas, petrol or any fuel which produces fumes. The fumes (vapour) will react, or burn, easily. Coal, however, must be heated to a very high temperature before it even starts to burn, unless the coal is in the form of a fine coal dust. Coal dust is dangerous as it can explode if a spark is produced nearby.

Where does energy come from?

The energy produced in the exothermic reactions described here comes from the chemicals themselves. Before the reaction has occurred, the chemicals both contain a certain amount of energy, and this energy is held there. If the two chemicals now react then some of the energy may be released.

This reaction can be shown in the example below:

Another important idea is that if you weighed all the acid and alkali then the mass of those two chemicals would equal the mass of the salt and water produced. In any chemical reaction the mass of the chemicals at the start of the reaction is equal to the mass of the new chemicals which are produced after the reaction has finished. The heat energy doesn't have a mass.

acid + alkali ➡ salt + water (energy released)		
total energy on this side	=	total energy on this side
total mass on this side	=	total mass on this side

about

Vinegar   Coke   Lemon juice   Orange juice

All the liquids in the picture above are acids.

What do these liquids have in common to make them all acidic? A simple experiment you can do is to test them all with universal indicator paper.

If you test them you will find that they all have a pH number less than 7. This is the first property that they all have in common.

The acidic pH scale

Substance	pH value
Acid in a car battery	1
Human stomach contents	2
Lemon juice	3
Vinegar	4
Acid rain	5
Coca cola	6
Tap water	7

The pH number tells you how strong an acid is. The closer the pH is to 1, the stronger the acid.

When acids come into contact with certain other substances they react and new substances are formed. One example of this type of behaviour you will probably see at school is where a metal like zinc or magnesium is added to an acid until it stops reacting. If the unused metal is extracted from the liquid by filtering and the liquid is heated to drive off the water, a white solid is left behind.

◀ *Magnesium metal reacts with sulphuric acid to produce magnesium sulphate.*

The white solid is a new substance produced by the reaction. In this particular case where magnesium has been added to sulphuric acid, the white substance is called magnesium sulphate.

The reaction can be described by the word equation:

magnesium + sulphuric acid ➡ magnesium sulphate + hydrogen

ACIDS

◄ *When magnesium reacts with sulphuric acid bubbles of hydrogen gas are produced.*

Making salts

Magnesium sulphate is a type of substance called a **salt**. When a metal displaces hydrogen gas from an acid the new substance formed is called a salt. The name of a salt is worked out from the name of the metal and the name of the acid, for example:

- zinc and hydrochloric acid produce a salt called zinc chloride
- iron and sulphuric acid produce a salt called iron sulphate
- magnesium and hydrochloric acid produce a salt called magnesium chloride

Salts can be made in other ways. One important method is to use a reaction called **neutralisation**. In this type of reaction you add a substance to the acid so it reacts to produce a salt and water. In some types of reaction the gas carbon dioxide is produced as well. Water has a pH of 7, so the result of the reaction is a neutral substance, hence the name neutralisation.

The substances that can be added to an acid to neutralise it are all called **bases**. Some different neutralisation reactions are:

Examples of neutralisation in everyday life

SOIL

Plants tend to grow best when the pH of soil is about neutral. Sometimes soil is too acidic, so calcium oxide (= a metal oxide) or calcium hydroxide (= a metal hydroxide) or calcium carbonate (= a metal carbonate) are added to the soil to neutralise it. You may have heard the common names for these substances:

- calcium oxide is commonly called quicklime
- calcium hydroxide is commonly called slaked lime
- calcium carbonate is commonly called chalk

NETTLE STINGS

Nettle stings are acidic. Calamine lotion contains a metal carbonate called zinc carbonate that can be used to ease the sting by neutralising the acid.

INDIGESTION

Your stomach contains acid to help you digest your food. If there is too much stomach acid it gets uncomfortable. The most common remedy for this is an indigestion tablet which is usually made from a carbonate that will neutralise the excess acid.

acid	+	metal oxide	➡	salt	+	water		
acid	+	metal hydroxide	➡	salt	+	water		
acid	+	metal carbonate	➡	salt	+	water	+	carbon dioxide

GALILEO, KEPLER and COPERNICUS

*G*alileo (1564–1642) was an Italian scientist. He was born in Pisa and lived there until the family moved to Florence when he was ten. He returned to Pisa in 1581 to study medicine at the university. By 1583 he had become interested in mathematics and physical science and started to study those subjects rather than medicine. He left the University of Pisa in 1585 without finishing his degree and spent the next seven years studying, writing and teaching either in Florence or in Pisa.

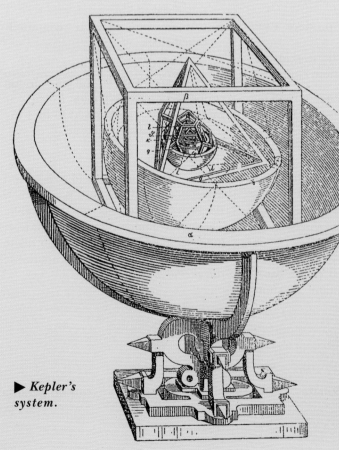

▶ *Kepler's system.*

In 1592 Galileo took a post as a professor of mathematics at the University of Padua. Five years later, he received the gift of a copy of a new book by a mathematics teacher at Grantz, in Austria, called Johannes Kepler. In this book, Mysterium cosmographicum (The cosmic mystery), Kepler explained a theory that the Universe was built around symmetrical figures with the Sun at the centre. This was the first public statement by any mathematician or scientist in support of the ideas of Copernicus (he thought that the Sun, rather than the Earth was at the centre of the Universe). Kepler had sent copies of his book to everyone he had heard of in the scientific world.

The problem was that the ideas of Aristotle and Ptolemy (they thought that the Earth was at the centre of the Universe) were firmly believed by most scholars. In spite of what Galileo agreed with Kepler, he did not publicly support Copernicus until 1613, 16 years later. Such is the power of public opinion!

THE COPERNICAN SYSTEM

opernicus (1473–1543) was a Polish priest. He studied mathematics at Cracow, astronomy at Bologna and medicine at Padua. He was trying to find a system of explaining the observations of the stars and planets that was more simple than the well-used system of Ptolemy. Over a period of 30 years or more he developed a theory of the way the planets moved. He believed the Sun was at the centre of their orbits, rather than the Earth being at the centre. Copernicus, as a Catholic priest, feared that because of his ideas he would be banned from the Church, so he delayed publication of his theory until he was dying. Although his book, published in 1543, contained the ideas that were to stimulate Kepler and Galileo, it was read by few people. The first edition of 1000 copies never sold out! The Copernican system was based on circles, but Kepler and Newton showed later that the paths of the planets are ellipses.

Copernicus was a theorist rather than an observer, but the impact of his ideas on Galileo and others was of major importance.

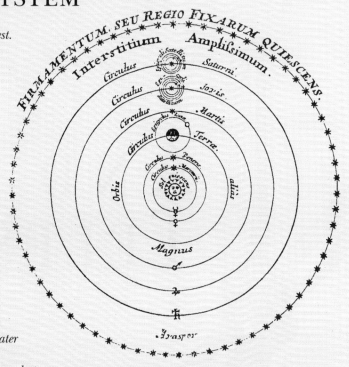

▲ *In the Copernican system the Sun is at the centre of the Universe with all of the planets orbiting round in circular motions. Copernicus's book* De Revolutionibus Orbium Caelestium *banned by the Church from 1616 to 1833 is now considered to be the first of the Age of Science.*

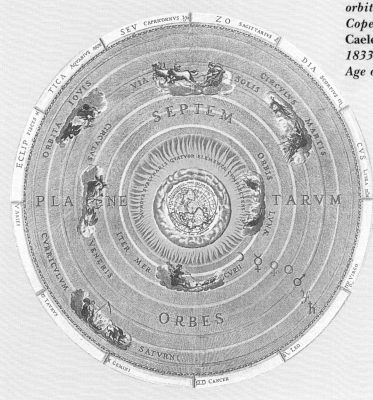

◀ *In Ptolemy's system (2AD) the Earth was at the centre of the Universe with its four elements earth, water, fire and air. The planets and the Sun were thought to move around the Earth in circular orbits.*

Galileo
AND HIS TELESCOPE

TVBVM·OPTICVM·VIDES·GALILAEII INVENTVM.ET OPVS,QVO SOLIS MACVLAS,
ET EXTIMOS LVNAE MONTES, ET IOVIS, SATELLITES,ET NOVAM QVASI
RERVM VNIVERSITATE PRIMVS DISPEXIT A. MDCIX.

▲ *Galileo built his first telescope in 1609.*

What made Galileo special was his use of observation and experiment to put ideas to the test. He was one of the first people to perform experiments in order to find things out.

Galileo's work with the telescope was fundamental in showing that the Copernican system was better than the ideas of Ptolemy. Galileo made a telescope after hearing rumours of an optical instrument invented in Holland that made distant things appear nearer. Although Galileo was famous for his work with the telescope he did not invent it. Nor could he explain how it worked! His telescopes were made by trial and error.

When Galileo looked at the planet Jupiter, he found he could see something new. He always recorded his observations carefully in a notebook. He had seen the moons of Jupiter. He realised that the 'small stars' were a set of moons moving around the planet. Sometimes they pass directly between the planet and the Earth. Sometimes they pass behind the planet (we say they are **eclipsed** by it).

Galileo's book *Siderius nuncius (The messenger of the stars)*, published in 1610, caused a sensation. First, it was short (24 pages) and easy to read: Copernicus' book *De revolutionibus* published 50 years earlier, and Kepler's book were difficult and read by only a few people. Second, Galileo's book described some of his telescopic observations of the Moon, stars and planets, and brought the arguments about the ancient view of the Universe out into the open.

▲ *Two of Jupiter's four moons are shown in the foreground. Io (left) is about 350 000 km above Jupiter's Great Red Spot. Europa (right) is about 600 000 km from Jupiter. This photograph was taken by Voyager I in 1979.*

MORE OBSERVATIONS

During the next three years Galileo made more observations, resulting in his first printed statement in favour of Copernicus, his *Letters on sunspots* published in 1613. Galileo's main observations with the telescope were as follows:

- The Moon has mountains and craters, and is not spherical and smooth and perfect as Ptolemy and Aristotle believed;
- The dark parts of the Moon are faintly lit up by light reflected from the Earth. Therefore, the Earth 'shines' when sunlight is reflected off it – just like other planets;
- Planets appear through the telescope as small discs, while stars look like pinpoints of light. So the stars must be a lot further away from the Earth than the planets are;
- The Milky Way is made up of a large number of clusters of stars;
- Venus has **phases** like the Moon: sometimes it looks like a crescent and sometimes like a complete disc. At those times when it looks like a disc it seems much smaller than when it looks like a crescent. So the distance between Venus and the Earth must change. The only possible explanation is that Venus moves around the Sun;
- Jupiter has four moons orbiting it. (We now know there are more, but Galileo could see only four with his telescope.) One of the objections to the Copernican system was its suggestion that the Moon orbited the Earth while everything else orbited the Sun. The motion of the Moon was, therefore, an **anomaly** – an imperfection. This suggested that the whole idea of the Copernican system must be wrong. People at that time believed that the heavens were perfect, so the idea of an anomaly really was a major objection. Galileo's observation showed that our Moon was not the only example of something moving around a planet;
- There are spots on the Sun, and their movement shows that the Sun rotates.

▲ *This is Galileo's sketch of Saturn. He thought that Saturn's rings were probably two moons. His telescope was not good enough to show them clearly.*

After publicising his theories and observations, Galileo was shunned by the Church and put into prison.

■ *For more about the planets see pp32–3.*

EARTHQUAKES

▶ *Quarrying (digging), mining and drilling have taught us a lot about what lies below the surface of the Earth, but these methods of exploration very rarely go deeper than about 10 km. If the Earth were the size of a tennis ball, the deepest oil well would correspond to a pinprick on the surface about as deep as the thickness of a piece of tissue paper. Humans have barely scratched the surface.*

inner core

outer core

crust

mantle

atmosphere

The Earth is a small rocky planet, which orbits a star called the Sun, in what is known as the solar system.

Inside the Earth

What we know about the Earth so far suggests that it has a layered structure rather like a cherry, as shown in the diagram on the left.

Scientists have learned about what the Earth is like inside, not so much from information from mines and oil wells, but from observing what happens during **earthquakes**. Earthquake activity shows an interesting pattern. This distribution and other observations have led geologists to believe

▼*The plates which make up the Earth's crust*

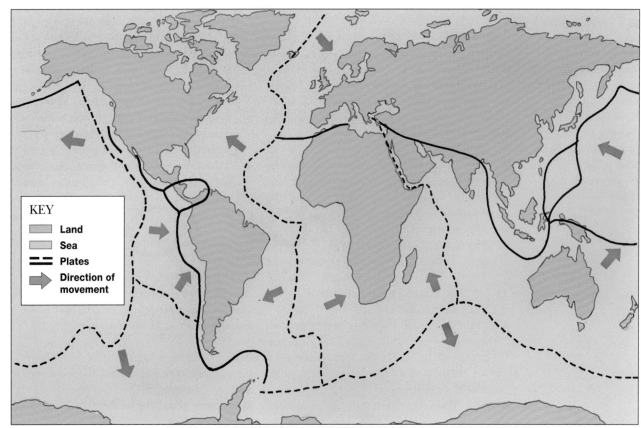

KEY

Land

Sea

Plates

Direction of movement

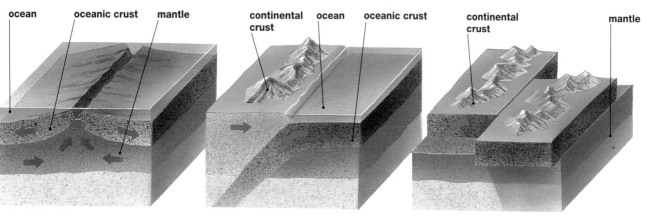

ocean | oceanic crust | mantle | continental crust | ocean | oceanic crust | continental crust | mantle

(a) One plate eases away from another. Magma rises to fill the gap and cools to form a ridge.

(b) The edge of the oceanic plate sinks under the continental plate. The crust melts and becomes part of the mantle.

(c) A fault is formed, e.g. the San Andreas fault in California.

▲ *Plates can (a) move apart, (b) collide, and (c) slide past each other.*

that the Earth's crust is made up of several enormous rigid **plates** of rock, up to 65-km thick. These plates are moving extremely slowly – at about the same speed, it is thought, that fingernails grow! Some are moving apart; some bump into each other or slide over each other.

arthquakes

When two plates collide, sometimes one plate ends up being forced beneath the other. This can cause a huge tear in the Earth's surface, called a **fault**. One of the best-known faults is the San Andreas fault, which marks the line along which the Pacific and the North American plates meet.

Even though the plates move very slowly, the rocks at their margins are under great pressure. There is enormous friction between the plates, sometimes the friction force is enough to stop the movement of the plates altogether. But the pressure gradually builds up so that eventually the rocks of the two plates tear apart with a sudden jolt, sending shock waves through the sur-

rounding rocks. If the jolt is great enough, the movement is felt at the Earth's surface. This movement is what we call an earthquake.

RECORDING EARTHQUAKES

Earthquakes are recorded by instruments which measure vibrations in the Earth's surface. Instruments called **seismographs** actually draw a graph showing the vibrations greatly amplified. The strength of an earthquake is measured on the **Richter scale**, which is drawn up in terms of the extent of these vibrations. Each unit on the Richter scale represents a tenfold increase in the strength of the vibrations – that is, an earthquake measuring 2 on the scale is 10 times stronger than one registering 1 on the scale. The most violent earthquakes ever recorded were at Quito, Ecuador, in 1906 and at Honshu, Japan, in 1933. Both measured 8.9 on the scale.

■ *For more about friction see pp28–9.*

SAN FRANCISCO'S EARTHQUAKES

Earthquakes can be extremely violent. Along the San Andreas fault there was a serious earthquake in the San Francisco area in 1906, which badly damaged the city, another in 1989 and one in 1993. These were caused by sudden slips of the Earth's surface along the fault.

D ID YOU KNOW?

There are many thousands of earthquakes each year, but only a very few are centred near towns or cities or are strong enough to cause loss of life. On average, between 10 000 and 20 000 people die from earthquakes every year. As a comparison, some 80 000 people are killed in road accidents each year in the United States alone.

VOLCANOES

There are about 850 active volcanoes in the world. The world's most devastating volcanic eruption occurred at Tambora in Indonesia in 1815 when 12 000 people were killed.

Volcanoes

When two of the plates of the Earth's crust move apart, molten (liquid) rock called **magma** can escape to the surface. Magma contains dissolved solids and gases; it is at a very high temperature and under great pressure. If there is any crack or weak point in the Earth's crust, magma is forced into it and sometimes makes its way through, pouring out on to the surface or being violently thrown into the air above. These ejections of magma are called **eruptions**. Magma, when it reaches the surface, is called **lava**. Lava builds up into landforms called **volcanoes**.

The shape of a volcano depends on the consistency of the magma.

Shield volcano

Magma that is thin and runny seeps through cracks in the crust more easily. Eruptions of this kind are gentler and the lava spreads out over a wider area, giving a broader, flatter volcano known as a **shield volcano**.

▼ *Mauna Loa in Hawaii is an example of a shield volcano.*

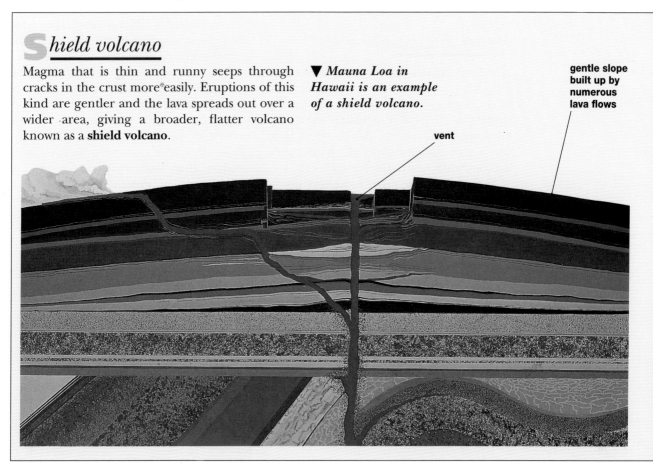

vent

gentle slope built up by numerous lava flows

Where volcanoes form

There are two types of plate margin at which volcanoes may form. At a **constructive plate margin**, two plates move apart and the gap between them fills with magma. Eruptions at constructive margins usually produce shield volcanoes. These are built up from runny lava often coming from several closely spaced points along the margin. At a **destructive plate margin** the plates slide over each other, and the rocks at the margin are melted by the intense heat produced by the frictional forces, forming magma. Volcanoes formed near destructive plate margins are usually conical in shape.

Fertile soils

Many people tend to live near volcanoes, despite their dangers. One of the reasons for this is that the soil around volcanoes is very fertile. The ash from volcanoes contains many nutrients, such as potassium, which plants need to grow.

DID YOU KNOW?

The word volcano comes from the latin name Volcanus, for the ancient god of fire.

Composite volcano

Thick, treacly magma is likely to solidify as soon as it reaches the surface and needs a greater force to eject it. The eruptions of treacle-like magma can be very violent, especially if it contains a lot of dissolved gas. The thick magma solidifies quickly, producing a tall **cone-shaped volcano** or **composite volcano**.

▼ *Mount Etna in Sicily is an example of a composite volcano.*

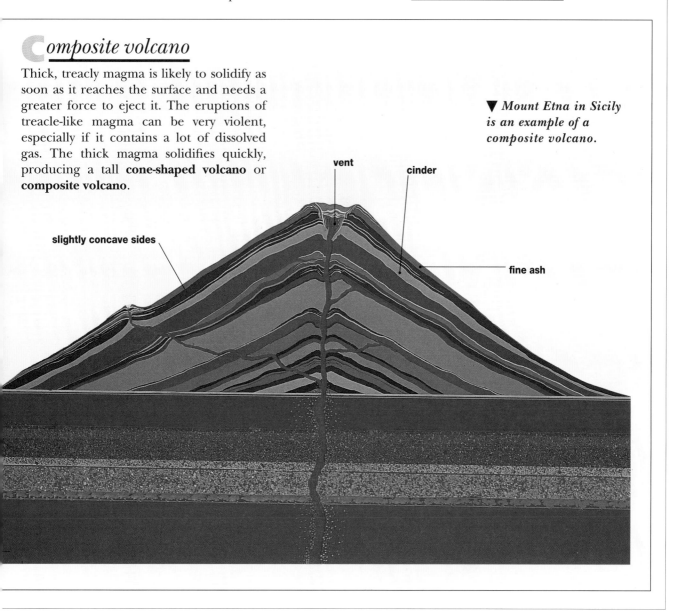

vent

cinder

slightly concave sides

fine ash

THE ROCK

These rock types are part of a slow cycle of matter called the **rock cycle.** *The Earth consists of three sections. There is a dense* **core** *surrounded by a liquid* **mantle** *and a thin* **crust** *on the outside.*

IGNEOUS ROCKS

Igneous rocks are formed when the molten magma from inside the Earth cools and turns solid.

Igneous granite

lava

METAMORPHIC ROCKS

Metamorphic rocks are produced by changing igneous or sedimentary rocks with pressure or heat.

An example of Lewisian gneiss

▲ *The rock cycle. This shows the recycling of rocks within the Earth's crust and mantle.*

CYCLE

SEDIMENTARY ROCKS

Sedimentary rocks are formed when eroded material is deposited on the floor of the sea and crushed together into new rock.

Sedimentary limestone

How rocks are formed

The central core of the Earth is very hot due to radioactive decay and this causes the molten magma to swirl about in slow convection currents. This movement of the magma causes the sections of the Earth's crust called **tectonic plates** to move slowly. When plates slip past each other, collide, or move apart various effects occur including earthquakes, volcanoes and the formation of new igneous rock. Igneous rock provides the source for the other two classes of rock, sedimentary and metamorphic. Sedimentary is formed when rock is eroded and broken down into smaller pieces that are carried away and deposited on the sea bed. Here they build up and harden into sedimentary rock. Metamorphic rocks are formed when rocks are affected by heat and pressure from igneous rocks.

■ *For more about tectonic plates see p91.*

new sedimentary layers forming

The PERIODIC TABLE

One of the most important skills in science is spotting patterns that can be used to make predictions.

A famous scientific collection of information that can be used to make predictions is called the **Periodic Table**. In the Periodic Table all the **elements** (substances made from only one type of atom) are arranged in order of the number of protons there are in the nucleus of a single atom (the **atomic number**) of the element. The elements are grouped so that there are eight vertical columns and a block of elements called the **transition elements**.

There are several significant patterns in the table:

- All the elements in the same group have the same number of electrons in their outer shell, for example lithium (Li), sodium (Na), and potassium (K), all have one electron on the outer shell and are known as the group I elements. Elements in group II have two electrons in the outer shell. Elements in group 0 have a full outer shell and do not react with other things. They are called the **inert** or **noble gases**.
- The properties of the elements in a group are similar and show a gradual change as you go down the group.

Group I elements

These are also called the **alkali metals** and they all react with water. The reaction with water gets more violent as you go down the group. Sodium melts as it reacts with water, but potassium bursts into flames as it reacts with water. The reactions between rubidium and water and caesium and water are even more dangerous. A piece of francium dropped into a large glass tank of water could produce an explosion which would probably destroy the tank!

GROUP

	I	II	
2	Li 3	Be 4	
3	Na 11	Mg 12	
4	K 19	Ca 20	Sc 21
5	Rb 39	Sr 38	Y 39
6	Cs 55	Ba 56	La 57
7	Fr 87	Ra 88	Ac 89

The Russian scientist Dmitri Ivanovitch Mendeleev (1834–1907) drew up the first version of the Periodic Table in 1869. He did this by charting the known chemical elements in order of increasing atomic mass, although we now know that it is the order of atomic numbers that is significant. He worked on the table, trying to improve it for several years. When Mendeleev was working on the table, only 63 elements were known, so he had to put some gaps in the table for missing elements. It was a stroke of genius to realise that some of the elements were missing! He used the patterns in the table to predict the properties of the missing elements. One of his most famous predictions, made in 1871, was about the element germanium (he called it eka-silicon). He said it would have properties somewhere between silicon and tin, that it would be 5.5 times heavier than water and it would form an oxide 4.7 times heavier than water. Fifteen years after he predicted it, germanium was found and Mendeleev was proved to be correct in his prediction.

Group 0 elements

This is a family of gases called the noble or inert gases. They are all very unreactive. Until about 30 years ago they were thought to be completely unreactive. But since then xenon has been made to react with flourine (from group VII).

Group VII elements

These are called the **halogens**. They are non-metals and become less reactive as you down the group. So fluorine is the most reactive, and so on. You may have heard the term halogen headlights. These use traces of some of these elements in the bulbs.

■ *For more about atoms see pp78–81.*

																		0
H 1																		He 2

			III	IV	V	VI	VII	
			B 5	C 6	N 7	O 8	F 9	Ne 10
			Al 13	Si 14	P 15	S 16	Cl 17	Ar 18

	Cr 24	Mn 25	Fe 26	Co 27	Ni 28	Cu 29	Zn 30	Ga 31	Ge 32	As 33	Se 34	Br 35	Kr 36
3													
b 1	Mo 42	Tc 43	Ru 44	Rh 45	Pd 46	Ag 47	Cd 48	In 49	Sn 50	Sb 51	Te 52	I 53	Xe 54
a 3	W 74	Re 75	Os 76	Ir 77	Pt 78	Au 79	Hg 80	Tl 81	Pb 82	Bi 83	Po 84	At 85	Rn 86

e 8	Pr 59	Nd 60	Pm 61	Sm 62	Eu 63	Gd 64	Tb 65	Dy 66	Ho 67	Er 68	Tm 69	Yb 70	Lu 71
h 0	Pa 91	U 92	Np 93	Pu 94	Am 95	Cm 96	Bk 97	Cf 98	Es 99	Fm 100	Md 101	No 102	Lr 103

▲ *The Periodic Table of elements. The horizontal lines are called* periods *and the vertical columns are called* groups.

◄ *metal element*

◄ *non-metal element*

METALS

Most of the elements are **metals**. If you look at the Periodic Table there is a line that zig-zags between the elements from the top of group III between boron and aluminium down to the bottom of groups VI and VII between polonium and astatine. The elements on the left of the line are metals. The elements on the right of the line are **non-metals**.

However, some of the elements next to the line like silicon and germanium have properties that are somewhere between metals and non-metals; these are called **metalloids**.

What properties do metals have in common?

- Metals are good conductors of heat and electricity;
- Most metals are **malleable** which means they can be hammered into different shapes;
- Metals are usually **ductile**, which means they can be pulled out into wires;
- Most metals have high boiling points and melting points; they are usually solid at room temperature (mercury is an exception to this);
- Metals are usually shiny;

Some metals are more reactive than others, but by comparing the way metals react with different substances, for example water, sulphuric acid and oxygen, we can produce a 'league table' of metals – the **Reactivity Series**.

Getting metals from rocks

Sometimes a lucky miner may find a lump (nugget) of gold. This only happens because gold is unreactive: it won't react with other substances in rock or soil. Most metals occur in nature as **compounds**. Compounds contain two or more elements

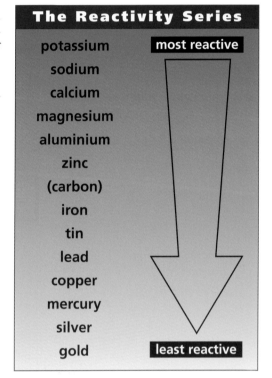

The Reactivity Series

most reactive

- potassium
- sodium
- calcium
- magnesium
- aluminium
- zinc
- (carbon)
- iron
- tin
- lead
- copper
- mercury
- silver
- gold

least reactive

chemically joined together. To get the metal from the compound you must separate it from other element(s). Sometimes you only have to heat the compound.

Competition between metals can be used to extract some metals. For example, titanium is separated from its compound, titanium chloride, by heating the compound with sodium metal. Sodium is more reactive than titanium. It combines with the chlorine to form sodium chloride, leaving the titanium uncombined. However, sodium is dangerous and expensive, therefore its use in this way is limited.

Some metals are obtained by other kinds of competition reaction. Iron is the most commonly produced metal. It is made by heating iron oxide (a compound of iron and oxygen) with carbon in a blast furnace. The carbon forms a compound called carbon monoxide which removes the oxygen from the iron oxide.

▼ *Molten iron in a blast furnace.*

and NON-METALS

The very reactive metals have to be separated from their compounds by using electricity. Usually the compound containing the required metal is melted, and a direct electric current is passed through it. Aluminium and sodium are both produced in this way.

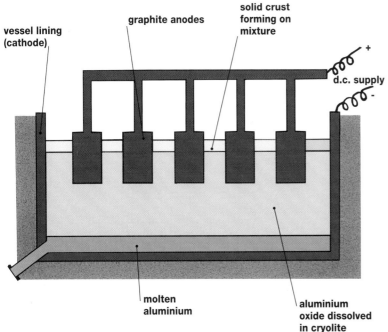

vessel lining (cathode)

graphite anodes

solid crust forming on mixture

+

d.c. supply

-

molten aluminium

aluminium oxide dissolved in cryolite

Extracting aluminium uses a lot of electricity. In the 19th century aluminium was very expensive. But once a way had been found to make electricity cheaply, aluminium became cheap enough to use for everyday things like milk bottle tops and saucepans.

◀ *Extraction of aluminium by electrolysis. Aluminium oxide has a high melting point and is not very soluble. However, it does dissolve in molten cryolite which is a compound of sodium, aluminium and fluorine.*

Density of metals

Suppose you have pieces of different metals that are all of the same volume – say a 1 cm³ cube. If you weigh them, you will find that their masses are all different.

This is because different metals are made of different kinds of atoms, and different kinds of atoms have different masses.

The mass of 1 m³ of a material is called the **density** of the material. The density of a metal is important in the use to which it is put. For example, magnesium and aluminium have low densities (that is, they are light metals) and are useful in the aircraft industry.

Alloys

Few metals are used in their pure state. Usually different metals are melted together to produce **alloys**. The properties of alloys differ from those of the metals they contain. Some are harder and stronger than the individual metals. Some resist corrosion better.

Some alloys are mixtures of metals with non-metals. Some of the most important alloys are steels because of their special properties like strength. Steels are alloys of iron with carbon, often with other metals, too.

METALS

Metals as catalysts

Some metals and alloys are **catalysts**. A catalyst alters the rate of a chemical reaction without itself being used up. Most industrial catalysts are used to speed up reactions that produce important chemicals.

Catalysts exist that can convert poisons in the exhaust gases from cars into harmless substances. These form part of the **catalytic converters** which are fitted in the exhaust systems of some cars.

DID YOU KNOW?

The so-called coinage metals have been chosen because they are strong, difficult to bend, resistant to wear so the design does not come off, cheap, easily pressed (stamped) with the coin design and resistant to corrosion.

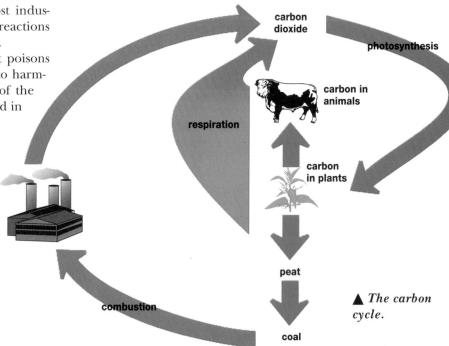

▲ *The carbon cycle.*

Properties of non-metals

Non-metals tend to have low melting points and boiling points, so many of them are gases or liquids at room temperature. Non-metals do not react with acids and do not conduct heat or electricity well.

CARBON

Carbon is one of the most important non-metals as it is the basis of all living things. The chemistry of carbon is called **organic chemistry**. Carbon is an interesting element. It occurs in two main forms when it is pure and these forms have very different properties. The two forms are called graphite and diamond.

Graphite is a soft black slippery solid that is a good conductor of heat and electricity. This is unusual as carbon is a non-metal

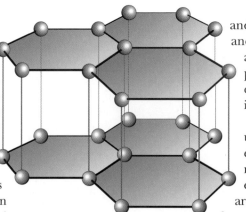

▲ *The structure of Graphite.*

and good conductors of heat and electricity are usually metals. The reason for these properties is the way the carbon atoms are arranged in the graphite.

Each carbon atom joins up with three others so that each sheet is based on a number of carbon rings joined together. These sheets are held together by weak forces and this makes graphite soft and slippery because the sheets can slide over each other. Each atom in the ring has an electron that is free to move through the lattice of atoms. These 'free' electrons make the graphite a good conductor of heat and electricity.

and NON-METALS

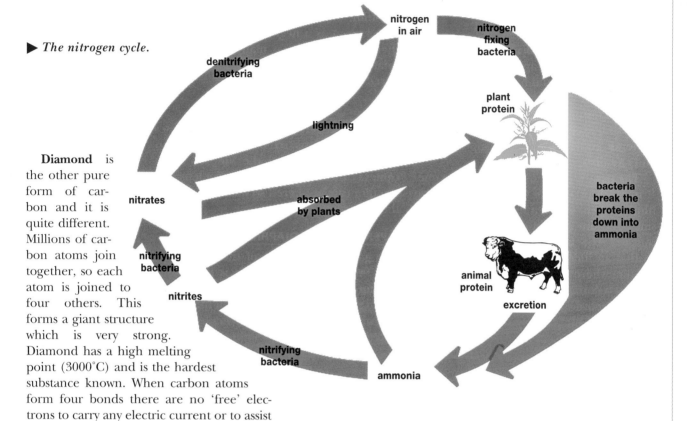

▶ *The nitrogen cycle.*

Labels in diagram: nitrogen in air, nitrogen fixing bacteria, denitrifying bacteria, plant protein, lightning, bacteria break the proteins down into ammonia, nitrates, absorbed by plants, nitrifying bacteria, nitrites, animal protein, excretion, nitrifying bacteria, ammonia

Diamond is the other pure form of carbon and it is quite different. Millions of carbon atoms join together, so each atom is joined to four others. This forms a giant structure which is very strong. Diamond has a high melting point (3000°C) and is the hardest substance known. When carbon atoms form four bonds there are no 'free' electrons to carry any electric current or to assist with heat conduction, so diamond is a poor conductor of heat and electricity.

Carbon is found in impure forms in coke, coal and charcoal, all of these are used as fuels. What makes carbon special is its ability to form long chains and rings. **Carbon chains** are the basis of substances like protein, fat, carbohydrate and of all living tissue.

NITROGEN

Several non-metal elements are gases at room temperature. Nitrogen, oxygen, argon, carbon dioxide and small traces of neon, helium, xenon and krypton make up the mixture we call air.

Nitrogen is a colourless gas that makes up four-fifths of the air. It has no smell, and it can combine with hydrogen to form a substance called ammonia which is the basis of a lot of household cleaners and of fertilisers used in agriculture.

Nitrogen is an essential element for living things. It is part of the compounds called proteins that make plants and animals. Plants and animals cannot get the nitrogen they need directly from the air. Plants get the nitrogen they need by absorbing substances called **nitrates** that are in the soil. Animals get the nitrogen they need by eating plants. These movements can be seen in the **nitrogen cycle**.

Of the 100 or so elements in the Periodic Table, less then one-fifth are non-metals, but they are very important. Without them we would not exist!

■ *For more about nitrates see pp58–9.*

D **ID YOU KNOW?**
About 2500 tonnes of nitrogen are produced in Britain each year. The gas is used for filling the spaces in oil tankers because it stops an explosive mixture of oil vapour and oxygen forming. It is used for filling food packages – liquid nitrogen has a boiling temperature of -196 °C which makes it useful for freezing foodstuffs.

The eye

The camera

The camera is an **optical instrument**. It is used to take photographs. Cameras can be very sophisticated and have a wide range of features such as automatic focussing, automatic exposure and automatic flash. They can also be very simple like the disposable cameras available in large supermarkets and chemists.

The basic idea of any camera is the same. It is a lightproof box with a light-sensitive film inside it. When a shutter is opened, a small amount of light enters the box from outside. The light passes through a lens so that an image of the outside forms on the film where the light changes the film to make a record.

The record can be made permanent by washing the film in certain solutions. The process of doing this is called **developing** the film. This produces a permanent picture known as a **negative**. The negative is then used to make as many copies of the final photograph as you want or are prepared to pay for.

LENS

Light from outside the camera passes through the **lens** so that a picture (an **image**) is **focussed** on the film. In many cameras, the distance between the lens and the film can be altered so that the focus of the picture is sharp.

APERTURE AND DIAPHRAGM

The gap in the middle of the **diaphragm** that the light goes through is called the **aperture**. The aperture needs to be wide on dull days so that it will let enough light in. On bright days the aperture is made smaller to reduce the amount of light let in.

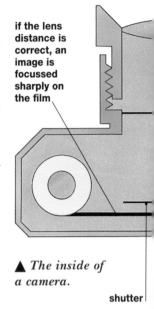

if the lens distance is correct, an image is focussed sharply on the film

▲ *The inside of a camera.*

shutter

The eye

The eye is a **sense organ** that is sensitive to light. It is much more sophisticated than any camera. There are some similarities and many differences. The main parts of the eye are shown in the diagram on the right. The **cornea** is the clear part in the front of the eye.

IRIS

Like the camera, the eye has a system for regulating the amount of light allowed to enter it. This is done by the **iris**. The iris is the part of the eye usually coloured either blue or brown.

Light can only pass through the circular hole in the middle of the iris – the **pupil**. Muscles in the iris control the size of the pupil. In dull conditions, the pupil is large to let enough light in and in brighter conditions the pupil is smaller to let less light in. This is similar to the diaphragm and aperture in the camera.

LENS

The **lens** in the eye is made of a jelly-like substance and the **ciliary muscles** control the shape of the lens. By altering the shape, the ciliary muscles let the eye focus on objects at different distances.

RETINA

The **retina** is an area of light-sensitive cells called rods and cones. Rods are sensitive to dim light and are used for black and white vision. Cones respond to bright light and can detect colour. The lens forms an image of the outside world on the retina and the **optic nerve** carries the information to the brain.

■ *For more about sight see p62.*

► *A cross-section of the eye.*

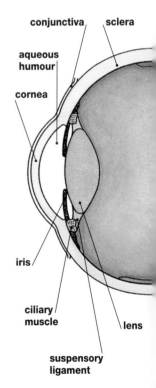

conjunctiva   sclera

aqueous humour

cornea

iris

ciliary muscle

lens

suspensory ligament

and the CAMERA

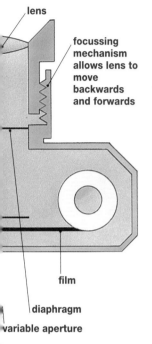

lens

focussing mechanism allows lens to move backwards and forwards

film

diaphragm

variable aperture

SHUTTER

The **shutter** is a gate that keeps the light out of the camera until the button is pressed to take the photograph. On advanced cameras the shutter speed can be varied to let more or less light in.

Typical shutter speeds allow light into a camera for about one-sixtieth of a second. If the shutter speed is longer than about one-thirtieth of a second then it may be difficult to hold the camera still enough to take the picture without using a **tripod**.

The shutter speed and aperture can be adjusted together on advanced cameras to let the correct amount of light on to the film. When the shutter cannot be set any slower and the aperture cannot be made any wider, then light from a **flash** has to be used to ensure a successful picture.

FILM

The **film** is a sheet of plastic coated with an **emulsion** which is sensitive to light. When light hits it, chemical changes take place. Developing the film converts these changes into a permanent negative that photographs can be made from.

Emulsions are made to have different sensitivities to light. The sensitivity is described by a number. Most common colour print films have numbers of either 100 ASA or 200 ASA (ASA is the unit for the film speed).

A film with a higher number is more sensitive to light and can be used in duller light than a film with a lower number. It can also be used with higher shutter speeds and, therefore, gives better pictures of objects that may be moving.

choroid

retina

vitreous humour

fovea

blind spot

optic nerve

THE APPEARANCE OF OBJECTS IN COLOURED LIGHT

Visible light has a continuous range of different wavelengths from about 0.0004 mm, which we see as violet to about 0.0007 mm which we see as red. The human eye responds to different wavelengths of light by 'seeing' the different colours.

White light is a mixture of all the wavelengths in the visible range. Coloured objects absorb certain colours and reflect others, but black objects absorb all colours and white objects reflect all colours. A red object reflects mainly red light and absorbs other colours. A red object can appear black in a blacked-out room if illuminated

with pure blue light. There is no red light to reflect and it absorbs the blue light. No light is reflected and so it looks black.

A related effect is the appearance of coloured clothing and carpets in shops. The colours of the materials can look quite different when taken outside if the fluorescent lighting in a shop has a slightly different combination of wavelengths from the sunlight outside. People who work with coloured wools and silks in embroidery often use a special daylight bulb to illuminate their work, which gives the same balance of wavelengths as sunlight.

Green

Cyan   Yellow

White

Blue   Magenta   Red

▲ *Mixing red, green and blue light produces white light.*

BEYOND THE

RAINBOW

In 1665 Isaac Newton was using a **prism** to split a beam of light into colours. He was trying to disprove the common believe of the time that colours were added to light by what it passed through. Newton had a different theory; he thought that when light passed through certain shapes of clear substance, like prisms or raindrops, the white light was split into its different parts. Newton was correct!

■ *For more about Newton see p32–3.*

▲ *The photograph shows a rainbow over Woolsthorpe Manor in Lincolnshire. This is where Isaac Newton was born on Christmas Day (25 December) 1642. He carried out the first thorough study of the colours of light.*

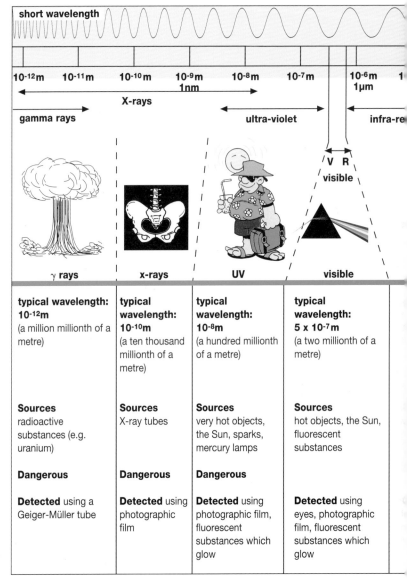

short wavelength

10^{-12}m	10^{-11}m	10^{-10}m	10^{-9}m	10^{-8}m	10^{-7}m	10^{-6}m	1
			1nm			1µm	

X-rays

gamma rays   ultra-violet   infra-re

V R
visible

γ rays	x-rays	UV	visible
typical wavelength: 10^{-12}m (a million millionth of a metre)	**typical wavelength:** 10^{-10}m (a ten thousand millionth of a metre)	**typical wavelength:** 10^{-8}m (a hundred millionth of a metre)	**typical wavelength:** 5×10^{-7}m (a two millionth of a metre)
Sources radioactive substances (e.g. uranium)	**Sources** X-ray tubes	**Sources** very hot objects, the Sun, sparks, mercury lamps	**Sources** hot objects, the Sun, fluorescent substances
Dangerous	**Dangerous**	**Dangerous**	
Detected using a Geiger-Müller tube	**Detected** using photographic film	**Detected** using photographic film, fluorescent substances which glow	**Detected** using eyes, photographic film, fluorescent substances which glow

Infra-red and ultra-violet

By 1802 it was known that there was some radiation that could not be seen on either side of the white light **spectrum**. Just beyond the red light there was a region where heat could be detected by a thermometer with a blackened bulb. This region was called **infra-red**. Just beyond the violet there was radiation which was invisible but affected reactions involving silver nitrate. This radiation was called **ultra-violet**. Both ultra-violet and infra-red radiations are outside the range of the human eye.

▼ *Sources and uses of the waves of the electromagnetic spectrum.*

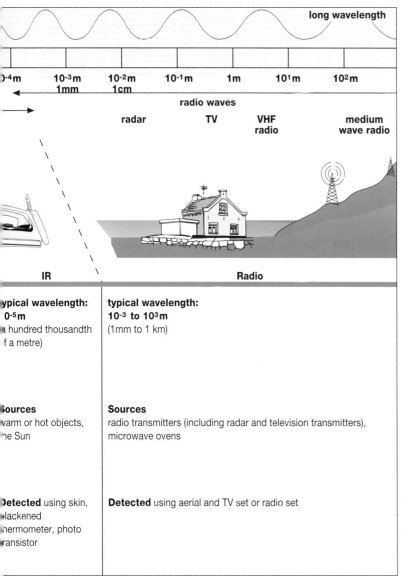

	typical wavelength:
ypical wavelength: 0⁻⁵m a hundred thousandth f a metre)	10⁻³ to 10³m (1mm to 1 km)
Sources varm or hot objects, he Sun	Sources radio transmitters (including radar and television transmitters), microwave ovens
Detected using skin, lackened hermometer, photo ransistor	Detected using aerial and TV set or radio set

Maxwell's Rainbow

The next important event came out of the work of James Clerk Maxwell. He produced a summary of everything known about electricity and magnetism in a scientific paper in 1864. He showed that the electric and magnetic effects produced by moving charged particles would spread through space like a wave. He also showed that this wave of magnetic and electric effects would travel with a particular speed. The speed he calculated was 300 000 000 ms^{-1}, the same speed as light waves travel. This suggested that light is an electromagnetic wave.

RADIO WAVES, X-RAYS, GAMMA RAYS AND MICROWAVES

Scientists then started to look for other types of electromagnetic waves apart from ultra-violet, infra-red and visible light. Radio waves were discovered in 1888 by Heinrich Hertz.

By 1930 X-rays, gamma rays and microwaves were all known. We now know the full electromagnetic spectrum, 'Maxwell's Rainbow' as it has been called. The important thing to realise is that the way we talk about the spectrum, by splitting it into regions, ignores the fact that it is continuous; there are no breaks.

Surrounded by waves

The waves of an electromagnetic spectrum surround us all the time. We can see only a very small part of the spectrum, but all of it is useful in different ways.

The Sun produces ultra-violet, infra-red and visible waves which are essential to the maintenance of life on Earth. X-rays and gamma rays have many uses in medicine and in giving us insights into regions where we cannot see.

The communications industry relies on vast areas of the spectrum through the radar and radio regions. Microwaves have many uses, especially in the kitchen. Imagine what life would be like without the waves beyond the rainbow!

■ *For more about electromagnetic waves see p16.*

COMMUNICATING *with* LIGHT

Light is a good way to send a message because it travels so fast. The warning that the Spanish Armada had been sighted was sent around England in 1588 by lighting beacons on hill tops. Each bonfire was visible from a long way away, and as soon as it was seen, the next beacon was lit to pass on the warning.

The problem with using light as a form of communication is that it is stopped by obstacles and won't go round corners, unless you set up some sort of mirror system. So the lamps that flash Morse code messages between ships can be used only where there is a direct line of sight.

Nowadays, however, light messages *do* go round corners! They travel along strands of glass called **optical fibres**. An optical fibre is very thin, like a hair, about one-tenth of a millimetre across. It is made of pure, clear glass. If the water of the English Channel were as clear as the glass in an optical fibre, you could look over the side of a cross-Channel ferry and see the sea bed!

■ *For more about optical fibres see p17.*

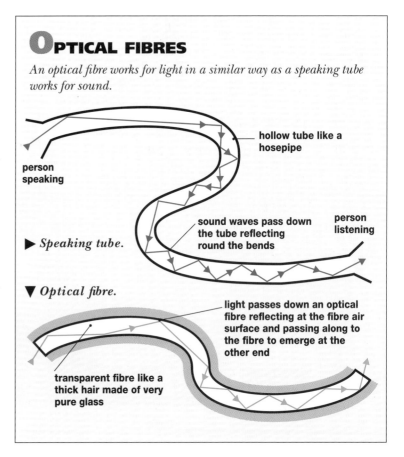

OPTICAL FIBRES

An optical fibre works for light in a similar way as a speaking tube works for sound.

hollow tube like a hosepipe

person speaking

▶ *Speaking tube.*

sound waves pass down the tube reflecting round the bends

person listening

▼ *Optical fibre.*

light passes down an optical fibre reflecting at the fibre air surface and passing along to the fibre to emerge at the other end

transparent fibre like a thick hair made of very pure glass

Sending messages

A **pulse** of light will pass from one end of an optical fibre to the other even if the fibre is bent. To pass a message down a fibre it has to be turned into a series of light pulses using a code that can be read at the receiving end of the fibre. Until recently telephone messages were coded into pulses of electricity and carried along copper cables. Optical fibres and light are now being used instead of copper cables and electricity in the telephone system.

WHY USE GLASS INSTEAD OF COPPER?

● Optical fibres are much lighter than copper cables;
● A signal will travel a long way down a

fibre before it starts to fade. A **repeater amplifier** is then used to boost the strength of the signal back up to the required level. A repeater amplifier is needed every 4 km for copper cable, every 100 km for optical fibres;

● If a copper cable passes near some other electrical appliance or cable, or if one cable picks up faint traces of the message travelling in the cable next to it, then interference can be picked up in the telephone calls. This is called **cross talk**. Cross talk does not happen with optical fibres;

● Optical fibres can transmit information at a much higher rate than copper wires. For example, an optical fibre link from

Luton to Milton Keynes can carry 140 million pieces of information *every second* without the need for a repeating amplifier.

There are some disadvantages to optical fibres, however.

- They are more difficult to join together than copper wires;
- They are more prone to break than copper cable;
- You can't send electrical currents down optical fibres to power the repeater amplifiers. (Why?) Copper wires, on the other hand, can carry electricity for both the amplifiers and the telephone signals at the same time. But few repeater amplifiers are needed for optical fibres so it is possible to give them their own power supply.

ANALOGUE SIGNALS

The telephone system converts the voice of a person into an **analogue signal**. This means that the signal size can be anywhere between zero and the maximum value.

Analogue signals can be transmitted down a wire by varying the size of the voltage, or down an optical fibre by varying the brightness of the light, in the same way as the sound volume varies.

DIGITAL SIGNALS

A better way of transmitting the message is to change the analogue signal into a **digital** signal. Digital signals are much easier to regenerate accurately when they start to fade. This gives a much better quality of sound.

A digital system uses only two values for all communication: high and low. If the digital system is an electrical one then the high and low can be two different voltage levels. If it is optical then the high and low could be the on and off of a light. The common way of representing these two states is by the numbers 1 and 0. High is represented by 1 and low is represented by 0. All information can be coded into a series of ones and zeros.

A TO D CONVERSION

Your voice is not digital, it is a continuously varying signal – an analogue signal. The process of coding an analogue signal into a digital signal is called **A to D conversion**. To represent your voice accurately as a digital signal, an A to D converter would have to produce a sequence of about 64 000 zeros or ones every second. (Each zero or one is called a **bit** which stands for **b**inary dig**it**.) A telephone system based on optical fibres may be able to handle 1 000 000 000 bits per second. So if one voice needs 64 000 bits per second, then the system can handle about 15 000 voices at the same time! A **multiplexer** prevents all the voices getting jumbled.

D TO A CONVERSION

At the receiving end of the telephone system the signal has to be converted back to an analogue signal so that our brains can interpret the information reaching our ears. Our hearing would not make sense of a digital signal! This process is called **D to A conversion**.

■ *For more about digital and analogue signals see p110–11.*

▼ *A to D and D to A conversion in the telephone system.*

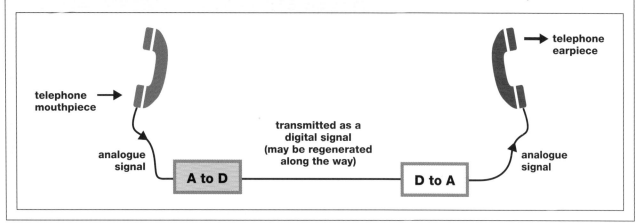

LASER
LIGHT

What is laser light?

Light produced by a **laser** is very pure. That is, it has a single colour and is made up of light waves that are all moving exactly together. For example, if a beam of ordinary light is like a queue of people walking down a road, then a beam of laser light is like an army of soldiers marching in step along the same road. As a result, laser light will stay in a narrow beam over very long distances. A laser beam can also be focussed into a very small spot, transferring a lot of energy into a tiny area.

If you focus light from the Sun (which isn't laser light) to a point, it will burn a hole in paper. With laser light you can do the same type of thing, but the focussed beam is powerful enough to burn a hole in a piece of metal!

■ *For more about lasers see p17.*

▲ *Focussed laser beams can cut through steel.*

Lasers in medicine

Lasers are used in medicine, often to destroy cells. This happens when a surgeon is treating a **tumour** (cancerous growth). A laser beam can be used like a scalpel. The beam affects only the cells in the top one-tenth of a millimetre of the surface it hits. So cancerous cells on the surface of, say, the throat can be burned off without damaging the cells underneath.

Lasers in supermarkets

Laser light is also used in many supermarket checkouts and large stores to read the **bar codes** printed on the things you buy.

The 'till' at the checkout is actually a **computer terminal**, called a point-of-sale terminal. All the terminals in the store are connected to a central computer. The central computer can be in the store, somewhere else, with the point-of-sale terminals communicating with it via a telephone. The price of every item in the store is programmed into the computer.

At the checkout, the goods are passed over a window, with a **scanner** below it. Low-power laser light is reflected off the bar code and back into the window of the scanner. The electronic system in the scanner interprets the reflection. It then communicates the information in the bar code to the point-of-sale terminal. (Sometimes the bar code reader is in the form of a 'wand' that is passed across the code.) The name of the item and its price are displayed, printed on the till roll and added to the bill.

Advantages of bar codes

One advantage of the bar code system to the store is that the staff don't need to put individual price labels on goods. Another advantage is that the main computer can use the information collected at the point-of-sale terminals to check stock levels, inform staff when shelves need refilling and report on how different goods are selling.

Using bar codes is supposed to be quicker than keying each item into the till by hand. But there is a risk that an item is scanned more than once, so you end up paying twice for the same thing. Systems are only as good as their operators!

▶ *Many supermarkets now use bar codes rather than keying in the price of the individual items.*

COMPACT

A compact disc is a digital recording. The original sounds have been coded into a signal that has only two values, high and low. This signal is stored on the disc.

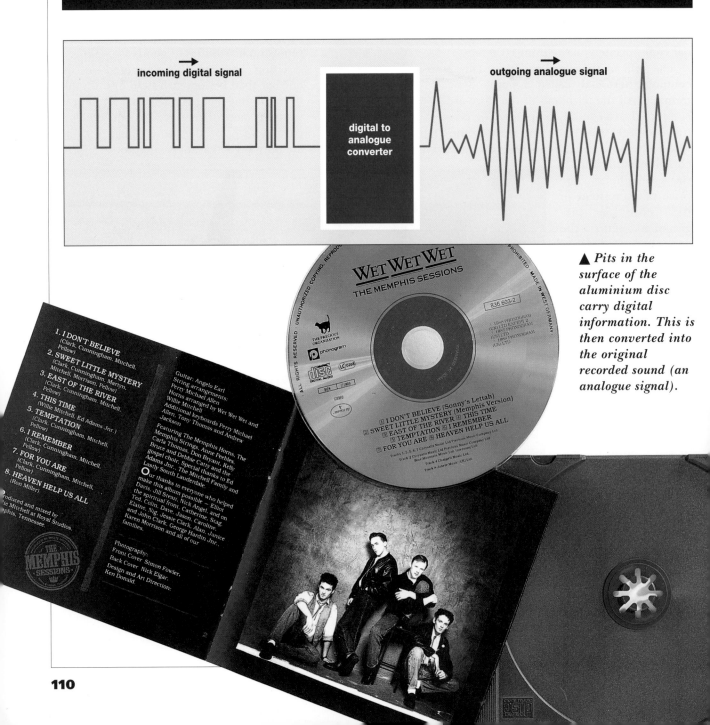

incoming digital signal

outgoing analogue signal

digital to analogue converter

▲ Pits in the surface of the aluminium disc carry digital information. This is then converted into the original recorded sound (an analogue signal).

DISC

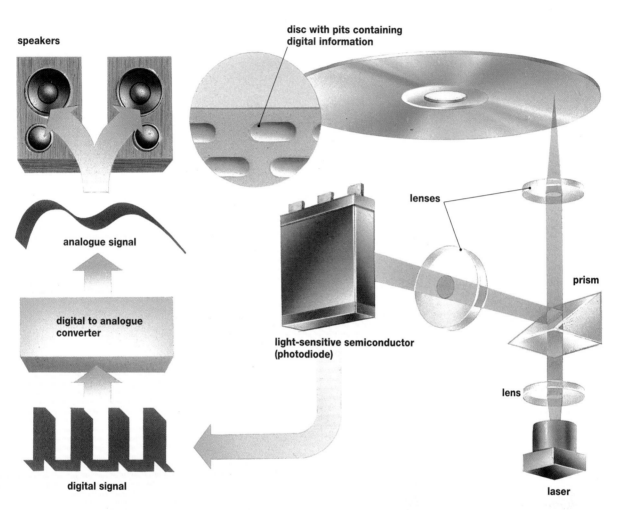

speakers

disc with pits containing digital information

analogue signal

digital to analogue converter

digital signal

light-sensitive semiconductor (photodiode)

lenses

prism

lens

laser

Music is recorded on the disc as a pattern of tiny pits on a layer of aluminium. The aluminium is protected by sealing it inside a clear layer of smooth plastic. When the disc is played, light from a laser is focussed on to it. The laser beam is reflected by the smooth aluminium but not by the rough surface of the pits. So the light reflected from the disc represents an exact copy of the pattern of pits on the disc. The reflected light is detected by a **photodiode.** This conducts electricity when light falls on it and does not conduct when there is no light.

The digital electrical signal from the photodiode is converted electronically to an analogue signal. This is amplified, and emerges as music from the loudspeakers.

The compact disc has several advantages over other kinds of recorded music. In particular, the high quality of the sound it produces does not deteriorate, however many times the disc is played. This is because the laser head does not come into contact with the disc and so will not 'wear out'.

■ *For more about analogue and digital signals see p106–7.*

ELECTRICITY WORKS

ELECTR✛STATICS

If you rub a plastic pen with a cotton duster the pen will attract small pieces of paper. It will also cause a thin stream of water coming out of a tap to bend.

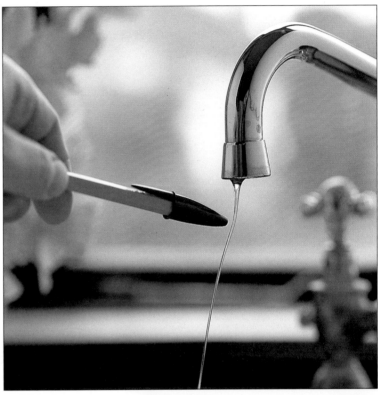

These effects occur because the pen has been given an **electrostatic charge** when it was rubbed on the cotton.

Electrostatic effects happen because there are two opposing types of charge. They are called **positive** and **negative** charges. Some ways of getting the two types of charge are shown in the table below.

▶ *Static electricity builds up on a plastic brush that is pulled through dry hair. The hair is also charged.*

Objects	Rubbed with	Charge on object
nylon	hair	positive
cellulose acetate (type of plastic)	cotton	positive
glass	silk	positive
polythene (type of plastic)	cotton	negative

all AR◉UND

Why does the pen get a charge?

The pen and the cloth, like all substances are made from atoms. Although there are many different types of atom, all atoms are made from a combination of three particles: electrons, protons and neutrons.

Electrons have a negative charge. Protons have a positive charge. Normally the cloth has equal numbers of protons and electrons (negative and positive charges) in it. So has the pen. So they are both neutral. When the cloth and pen are rubbed together some of the electrons from the cloth transfer on to the pen. This leaves the pen with some extra electrons (a negative charge). The cloth is left with some protons which have no electrons to neutralise them (a positive charge).

Remember, though, when two substances are rubbed together, it is *only the electrons* that can transfer.

THE LAWS OF ELECTROSTATICS

Experiments with different charges show that:

● *Like charges (+ and +, or - and -) repel each other;*
● *Unlike charges (+ and -) attract each other;*
● *If two positive charges are brought together their combined effect is like a larger positive charge;*
● *If two negative charges are brought together their combined effect is like a larger negative charge;*
● *If a negative charge and a positive charge are brought together their effects cancel each other. If the two charges are exactly the same size, the result of bringing them together is to cancel out the effects completely. The result is something that has no charge. We say it is* **neutral**.

When electrons are transferred between substances by friction (rubbing), they can get stranded for a long time in their new places. The negative and the positive charges that result are called electrostatic charges.

For example, if you walk on a nylon carpet, electrons rub off the carpet and on to you. You can build up quite a large negative charge of **static electricity**. You do not realise it unless you touch a **conductor**, such as a metal object in contact with the ground. This lets all of the electrons rush away from you and into the ground, and you get a small electric shock.

Electrostatics was one of the first aspects of electricity that scientists investigated. For many years it was regarded as having no practical use. It was used only for party tricks and amusement. Today there are many uses of electrostatics.

■ *For more about electrostatics see p114–15.*

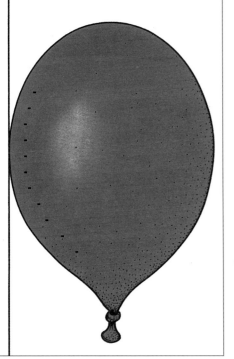

◀ *You can charge a balloon by rubbing it on a woollen sweater. If you hold the negatively charged balloon to the wall it will induce an opposite charge on the wall by repelling the electrons away from the surface of the wall. The negatively charged balloon is then attracted to the positively charged wall surface.*

APPLICATIONS *of*

In today's world there are many important uses of electrostatics.

The Van de Graaff generator

In schools a Van de Graaff generator is used to demonstrate some of the effects of high charges. Larger versions of the machine are used to find out more about the particles inside atoms.

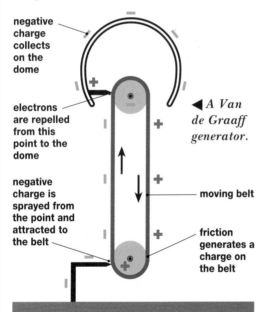

negative charge collects on the dome

electrons are repelled from this point to the dome

negative charge is sprayed from the point and attracted to the belt

◀ *A Van de Graaff generator.*

moving belt

friction generates a charge on the belt

A Van de Graaff generator can be used to accelerate charged particles to the high speeds needed to break up other particles with which they collide. The results of the collisions can tell scientists a lot about the make-up of particles.

■ *For more about atoms see p78–81.*

▶ *Positively charged thin wires are stretched across the centre of the chimney. They cause the gas around them to be charged. Because of this, the smoke particles become positively charged. The positive particles are then repelled by the wires, towards the earthed metal plates, where the dust sticks. A mechanical hammer hits the plates every few minutes and the ash falls down into a bin. It is then used to make house bricks.*

F IRE HAZARDS

An electrostatic spark can cause an explosion where fuels and other highly flammable substances are used.

Aircraft tyres are made from a special rubber that will conduct electricity. When an aircraft flies through the air electric charges can build up on it, due to friction with the air. A spark on touchdown could be disastrous because it could ignite the aviation fuel. The tyres allow the charge to be neutralised without a spark. This also means that the passengers won't get a shock when they step off the plane.

P ollution control

A power station that uses coal as its energy source can produce about 30 000 kg of ash every hour. A lot of this ash will be carried out into the air from the chimneys to pollute the environment, unless something is done to stop it. **Electrostatic precipitators** remove about 99 per cent of the ash before the smoke goes up the chimney.

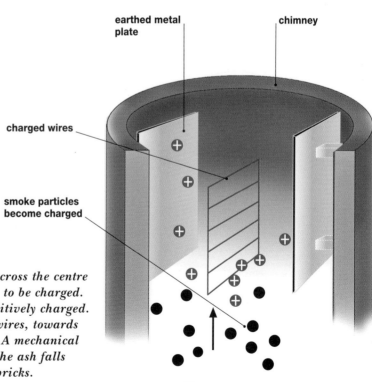

earthed metal plate

chimney

charged wires

smoke particles become charged

ELECTROSTATICS

The photocopier

The photocopier works by electrostatic charging. A vital part of the machine is a large **drum**, which is charged by having a wire at a high voltage near to its surface.

The document for photocopying is placed on a glass sheet and the photocopier lid is closed. When the button is pressed to start the printing a very bright light passes over the face of the document. The light reflected from the surface of the document is guided by a system of mirrors and lenses so that it forms an image of the document on the drum.

FORMING THE IMAGE

The image is formed in a clever way. Before the light hits the drum, the drum has a positive charge all over it, because it has passed close to the high-voltage wire. Where the light is focussed on the drum the charge is neutralised. So parts of the drum left with a positive charge correspond to the dark parts of the original document.

A black powder **toner** is given a negative charge by the machine and dusted on to the drum. Because of its charge, the toner is attracted on to the positively charged sections of the drum.

The drum now carries an exact copy of the original document. If the photocopier has an adjustable lens system then it is possible for the copy to be a different size from the original. It may be larger (an enlargement) or smaller (a reduction).

The photocopying paper is then rolled under the drum. A wire under the paper is given a charge, and this attracts the toner off the drum and on to the paper. The paper, carrying the toner, is then passed through heated rollers. This makes the toner stick to the paper, creating a permanent copy.

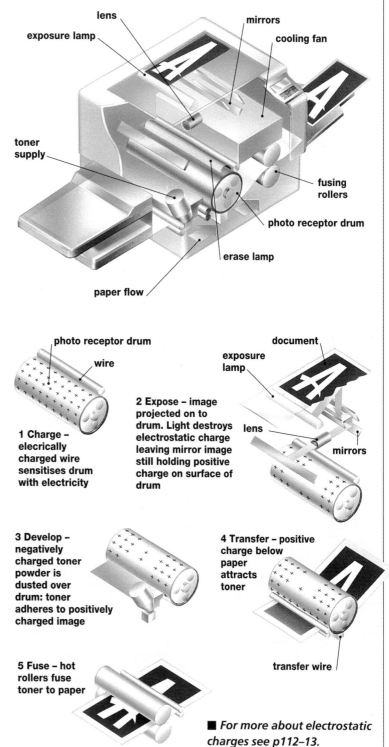

1 Charge – elecrically charged wire sensitises drum with electricity

2 Expose – image projected on to drum. Light destroys electrostatic charge leaving mirror image still holding positive charge on surface of drum

3 Develop – negatively charged toner powder is dusted over drum: toner adheres to positively charged image

4 Transfer – positive charge below paper attracts toner

5 Fuse – hot rollers fuse toner to paper

■ *For more about electrostatic charges see p112–13.*

THUNDER

An American inventor, Benjamin Franklin, is famous for flying a kite in a thunderstorm to see if lightning is caused by electric charges in the thunder clouds. He knew that if he held his knuckle near to a highly charged rod, a small spark would be produced. When he flew the kite into a thunder cloud he saw a spark jump between a key tied to the kite string and his knuckle. An electric charge had moved down the string to the key to produce the spark. The charge was coming from the thunder cloud.

We now know that there are massive charges (hundreds of thousands of coulombs) in thunder clouds and that Franklin was very lucky to survive! Another scientist was killed trying to repeat the experiment.

Measuring the charges

In the 1930s scientists studied the charges in thunder clouds by safer methods. Measuring instruments were attached to balloons and the balloons set free to rise up

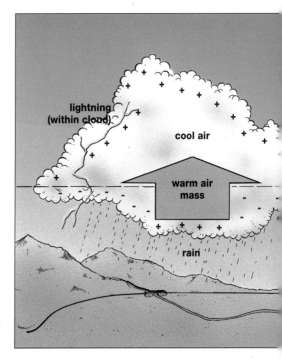

through the clouds. At a certain height, the instruments were released from the balloon and returned to the ground by parachute. The measurements showed that the charges in the clouds were distributed as shown in the picure above.

Lightning

Lightning occurs when the air **molecules** can no longer insulate the charges from each other. Most lightning happens within the cloud itself. This appears as a general glow called **sheet lightning**.

When lightning strikes the ground an electric current passes through the air between the cloud and the ground so that the cloud becomes **discharged**. The current causes the air to glow and this is what we see as lightning. Photographs of lightning taken with special cameras show that there

*B*enjamin Franklin (1706–90) was an American printer, scientist, publisher and statesman who played an important role in the formation of the United States as a nation. Franklin helped draft the Declaration of Independence and signed the Constitution. He was born in Boston, Massachusetts, the tenth son of 17 children. When he was 12 years old he went to work for his brother, a printer, but gave it up in 1748 to study science. He proved that lightning was electrical and later invented the lightning conductor to protect buildings. He also invented bifocal glasses and a smokeless stove.

and Lightning

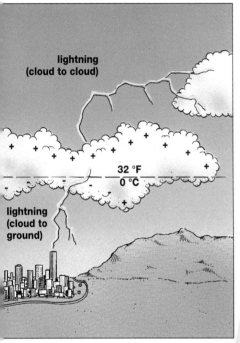

▲ *The formation of lightning.*

are different sorts of lightning. Sometimes there is just a single lightning stroke. Sometimes a series of strokes, perhaps a dozen or more, follow each other along the same track within a few hundredths of a second. To the naked eye, they look like a single flash.

The current in a lightning flash is usually about 10 000 A but it can be as much as 100 000 A.

A lot of energy is transferred in a lightning flash – perhaps 10 000 000 000 J. Some of this energy heats up the air in the flash to about 30 000 °C. The air expands very fast indeed, creating the sound waves that we hear as thunder.

What is a lightning conductor?

The **lightning conductor** is used to stop a building being hit by lightning. It works in the same way that an earthed needle stops a Van de Graaff generator from sparking.

The lightning conductor is a sharp, pointed rod connected to a plate in the ground. When the negatively charged base of a thunder cloud is over it, the electrons in the conductor are repelled down into the earth. So the point of the conductor becomes positively charged. The lightning is therefore more likely to strike the conductor than anything else in the area, and flow safely to earth.

How far away is a thunderstorm?

Light travels about a million times faster than sound. The light from a lightning flash will cover several kilometres almost instantly. The sound of the thunder, which is the noise made by the energy transferred in a lightning flash, travels at about one-third of a kilometre per second. So, if you see a lightning flash and hear the thunder three seconds later, you are about a kilometre away from the storm.

▲ *This bolt of lightning was triggered by a small research rocket. Smoke from the rocket's engine is seen illuminated by the lightning. The rocket is launched into a thunderstorm trailing a copper wire, which the lightning uses to reach earth. Researchers can use this technique to measure the current and voltage of lightning strikes.*

WHAT is electricity?

Many people think that electricity is 'what comes out of a plug' when an appliance is plugged into the mains. In the everyday world that is probably all that most of us need to know, but it is neither very accurate nor very useful, especially in science. 'What comes out of a plug' is actually an electric current, but to understand what that is you need to understand a few other ideas first like 'charge', 'particle' and 'conductor'.

Particle

In science the word **particle** is used for something that is so tiny that you cannot see it. In fact, the things that scientists refer to as particles are so small they are thought of as having no effective volume at all. There are many different particles and some are made up of special groupings of other particles. Eventually, when you get millions and millions of these particles into groups you start to get pieces of matter that can be seen.

Particles you hear about in science include protons, electrons, neutrons, atoms and molecules. Atoms are made up from combinations of protons, neutrons and electrons (except for hydrogen atoms which do not contain any neutrons). Molecules are made up from groups of atoms bonded together in certain ways. The objects that make up our world are made from millions and millions of such particles.

■ *For more about atoms see p78–81.*

Charge

Some of these particles have a property we call charge. There are two types of charge, positive and negative. The particles called protons have a positive charge and the particles called electrons have a negative charge. When something does not have a charge at all it is said to be neutral. The

the battery pushes electrons around the circuit

battery

resistance

the resistance determines the speed of flow of electrons

most of the electrical energy is transferred into heat energy **HEAT**

particle that is called the neutron is neutral. If you have equal amounts of positively and negatively charged particles mixed together, the effects of the charges cancel out. Most everyday objects are neutral because they contain equal numbers of protons and electrons. In some circumstances you can make a substance gain or lose a few electrons so that it becomes charged and you can see the effects. The

A lessandro Volta (1745–1827) was an Italian scientist. In 1794 he explained why a frog's leg twitched when its muscles were touched with two different metals. This happened because an electric potential difference was produced between the two metals. Potential difference occurs when there is a difference in charge between two points. Volta made the first battery in 1800.

◄ *Alessandro Volta demonstrating his battery to Napoleon.*

effect of the unbalanced charges have been noticed and studied for hundreds of years. The study of them is called electrostatics or static electricity.

■ *For more about electrostatics see p112–15.*

Conductor

Metals and carbon will allow electrons to pass through them. A substance that allows charges to pass through it is called a **conductor**. The flow of charge through a conductor is called an **electric current**. **Batteries** and generators are devices that will push electrons round a complete circuit made from conducting materials.

■ *For more about generators see p128–9.*

Circuit

The flow of charge, or current, is measured in amps. When a current of 1 A is flowing in a circuit, there are about 6 million million million electrons passing a point in the circuit every second. The charge is not 'used up' as it goes round the circuit. It is a bit like the water that flows around a central heating system: it is not used up, it just keeps going round and round as the pump moves it. The battery in a circuit is a bit like an electron pump.

Moving charges

When charges move they produce three different effects. First, whatever they move through heats up. This effect is the basis of light bulbs with **filaments**, electric fires, toasters and electric kettles. Second, they produce magnetic effects around the wire. This effect is the basis of the electric motor and hence food processors, vacuum cleaners, CD and tape players. Third, they can cause certain substances to change chemically when the charge passes through them. This is the basis of the battery charger.

The study of moving charges and their effects is called **current electricity**.

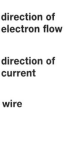

electron

↑ direction of electron flow

↓ direction of current

wire

▲ *For electrical energy to flow there must be a complete circuit.*

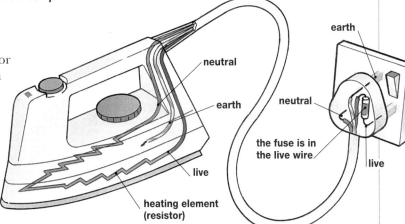

earth

neutral

earth

neutral

the fuse is in the live wire

live

live

heating element (resistor)

▲ *When you plug something into the mains, there is a flow of charge into and out of the appliance through the plug.*

MAGNETS *and*

Since ancient times many people have been interested in lodestone, because it will attract small pieces of iron. Lodestone is actually a type of iron ore. Its proper name is magnetite.

The name **lodestone** comes from the old Anglo-Saxon word *lode* meaning 'way'. If a piece of lodestone is suspended so that it is free to turn, it will always settle so that the same part of it points to the north. The lodestone was the first type of compass used by travellers. It made it possible for ships to navigate through mist and fog when neither the Sun nor the stars were visible.

Other substances will also attract small pieces of iron. Pieces of substance that do this are called **magnets**. Magnets can be made only of certain materials. The only metal elements that are magnetic are cobalt, nickel and iron. Substances that are made from these metals may also be magnetic. A good example is steel, which is made from iron and carbon.

Like lodestone, a magnet will line up pointing to the magnetic north pole of the Earth (if it is free to turn). The part of a magnet that points to the north is called **north-seeking pole**. This is usually shortened to **north pole**. The part of a magnet that points to the south is called the **south pole (south-seeking pole)**.

▶**1** *In one experiment Gilbert floated a piece of lodestone on water. He did this by putting his lodestone on to wood and floating the wood on the surface of the water.*

*A*s far as we know, the first person to study magnets scientifically was an English doctor called William Gilbert (1540–1603) whose book on magnets was published in 1600. Gilbert was physician to Elizabeth I and James I. His experiments can be repeated easily with small bar magnets, but he used small lodestones on which he made marks to show the poles.

In other experiments Gilbert showed that if a magnet is divided into pieces then pairs of new poles are created at the breaks. It is impossible to isolate a north pole. There is always a south pole paired with it.

▲**2** *Then he held another piece of lodestone near the first so that the two pieces had their north poles close to each other. He found that the floating lodestone was pushed away from the held lodestone.*

◀**3** *He repeated this experiment to find out what happened when two south poles were near each other. They also pushed each other apart. But when a south pole was brought close to a north pole, the pieces of lodestone attracted each other (pulled each other together). He had discovered an important law of magnetism:* poles that are the same push each other apart; poles that are different attract each other.

MAGNETISM

How to MAKE A MAGNET

One way to make a magnet out of a piece of steel is to stroke the steel repeatedly from one end to the other with a magnet. You must always use the same end of the magnet to stroke with, and always stroke the steel in the same direction.

Domains

To explain the behaviour of magnets, scientists have suggested that every atom is like a small magnet. In some substances like iron these small atomic magnets form into tiny groups called **domains**. Usually the domains lie in all directions and their effects cancel out. But if the domains can be made to line up pointing in the same direction they all work together to produce a magnetic effect. The substance can therefore be made into a magnet.

Did You Know?

The name 'magnet' comes from the name of the city of Magnesia in Asia Minor, where iron ore was mined in the time of the ancient Greeks.

Curie temperature

The domain theory of magnets can be used to explain the effect of heat on magnets. At a certain temperature called the **Curie temperature**, which is different for different substances, a magnet will lose its magnetism. The theory says that at the Curie temperature the vibration of the atoms in the domains becomes so vigorous that they stop pointing in similar directions and the domains cease to exist. An alloy containing 70 per cent of nickel and 30 per cent of copper has a Curie temperature of about 70 °C.

Did You Know?

The effect of heat on magnets was discovered by Marie Curie's husband, Pierre, after whom the Curie temperature is named. The Curie temperature of iron is 760 °C.

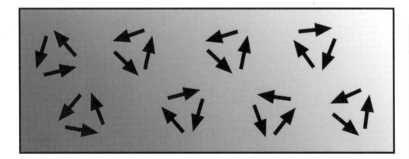

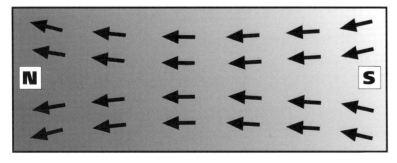

◀ *An unmagnetised piece of steel has domains lying in all directions (top). When it is magnetised, the domains line up in the same direction (bottom).*

MAGNETS *and*

The compass

The first compasses were made from lodestone. Now better compasses can be made using a steel needle on a pivot. People used to think that one end of the compass was attracted to the Pole Star, but it was realised later that the Earth itself behaves like a giant magnet. The north (north-seeking) end of the compass is attracted to the Earth's magnetic north pole. The south (south-seeking) end of the compass is attracted to the Earth's magnetic south pole. The magnetic poles are close to, but not the same as the north and south geographic poles.

◀ An early mariner's compass in a wooden bowl. This was made in about 1750.

true north

magnetic north

Angle of declination

The direction in which the compass points is affected by the presence of certain types of rocks and ores in the Earth's crust. This means that the angle between the true north and the direction in which the compass points varies from place to place over the Earth's surface. The angle between the compass direction and the north is called the **angle of declination**.

The angle of declination also changes year by year because the positions of the Earth's magnetic poles alter as time goes by.

S

N

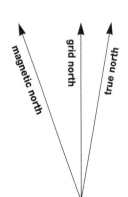

magnetic north   grid north   true north

▶ *On an ordnance survey map you will see three norths: magnetic north which varies with place and time, grid north and true, or geographic north.*

DID YOU KNOW?

The magnetic north pole of the Earth was first reached by an explorer in 1831. The south magnetic pole was not reached until 1909, when it was located by one of Sir Ernest Shackleton's expeditions.

MAGNETISM

▼ *The Earth is like an enormous magnet. Its North Pole is actually a magnetic south pole and the north poles of magnets are attracted to it. The poles of the magnet are not exactly at the geographical North and South poles, but are just a few degrees away.*

Angle of dip

As well as pointing towards the magnetic north, the compass also points down into the Earth in the northern hemisphere and up out of the Earth in the southern hemisphere. You can see this effect if you suspend a compass needle so that it is free to turn in a vertical circle.

The effect is due to the pattern made by the Earth's magnetic field. It means that the ordinary magnetic compass does not work very well where the **angle of dip** is high (more than 80°).

In Britain the angle of dip is about 70°. This means that a steel bar can be magnetised by holding it so that it points towards the magnetic north and downwards at 70° and then hammering it. The Earth's magnetic field lines up the domains in the steel bar along its length as it vibrates, turning it into a magnet.

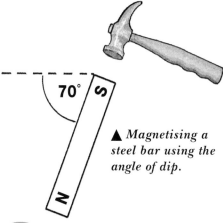

▲ *Magnetising a steel bar using the angle of dip.*

Gyroscopic compass

Ships and aircraft now use a **gyroscopic compass**. This is a spinning disc; once it has been set spinning, it will always point in the same direction. The gyro-compass is set spinning so that it points north and then it is kept spinning. Because it does not rely on the Earth's magnetism, it is not affected by changes in the angles of declination or dip.

DID YOU KNOW?

The steel hull of a ship becomes magnetised by hammering when it is built. So the compass in a ship always has to have correcting magnets near it, to cancel out the effect of the ship's magnetism.

▼ *This gyroscope has been set spinning on the point of a pencil. Once it has been set spinning it will retain its position exactly as long as it keeps spinning.*

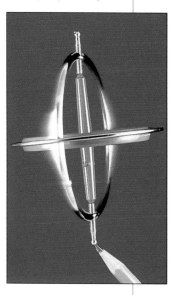

DID YOU KNOW?

Polos is the Greek word for pivot. The name 'pole' comes from this word. The Pole Star is on the line of the Earth's axis. When the Earth turns, it seems to us that the whole Universe pivots about the Pole Star.

Michael Faraday

Michael Faraday was responsible for inventing several important electrical devices including the dynamo, the electric motor and the transformer. Two units in electrostatics, the farad and the faraday, are named after him.

Michael Faraday (1791–1867) was born in Surrey. He was the son of a blacksmith. Although he had little education other than basic English and Maths he eventually became one of the greatest experimental scientists the world has ever known. His first job was as an errand boy for a bookseller, and while he was there, he started reading some of the articles in *Encyclopaedia Britannica* and decided to teach himself to improve his reading and writing.

One of the bookshop customers took young Faraday to hear a science lecture given by Sir Humphry Davy. Davy was a very important figure in the science world at the time. After the lecture, Faraday wrote to Davy asking if he could work with Davy at the Royal Institution, the centre for scientific study in London.

When Faraday was 21, Davy offered him a job as a laboratory assistant at the Royal Institution. Later that year, Faraday went with Davy on a tour of Europe, meeting all the leading scientists of the day.

Electromagnetism discovered

In 1820 the scientific world became interested in electricity and magnetism following a discovery of the 'link' between them by the Dutch scientist Hans Christian Oersted. Although Oersted had been working since 1807 to find a link between electricity and magnetism, he actually found it

quite by accident! While demonstrating something else, he put a compass on top of a wire that had a current flowing down it. He noticed that the needle moved so that it pointed at right angles to the wire.

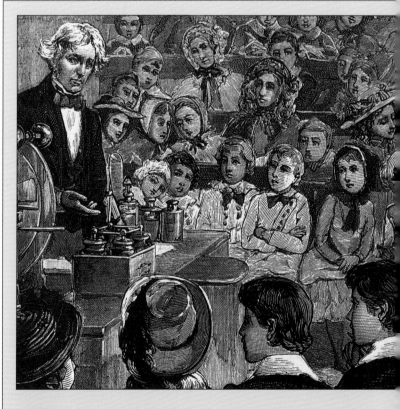

Faraday used to give lectures in the lecture theatre in the Royal Institution. He started the Christmas lectures for children. They still continue today, and some very famous scientists have taken part. You may be able to watch them on television.

He had discovered that there was a magnetic field around a wire carrying an electric current!

When news of this discovery became public many important discoveries and inventions followed. Within three years, the **galvanometer** (a current detector) was invented, André-Marie Ampère showed that current-carrying wires will attract or repel each other depending on the current directions, and the first **electromagnet** was built by William Sturgeon. In 1821 Faraday made the first electric motor.

By this time Faraday lived in a flat above the Royal Institution. Over the next 30 years Faraday carried out thousands of experiments, which he wrote up in his diary. The records of his experiments were published in several volumes. If you live near a large reference library or if you can visit the Science Museum in London, you may be able to see some of Faraday's work.

Faraday's experiments

Faraday made his most famous discovery on 29 August, 1831. He did not totally understand what he had found at first and spent most of the following six months in follow-up experiments. Faraday had performed the following magnet-in-coil experiment:

▶ *When the magnet was moved downwards into the coil the current in the coil flowed one way.*

▶ *When the magnet was stationary within the coil there was no current flowing.*

▶ *When the magnet was taken out of the coil the current flowed in the opposite direction.*

Faraday was a great experimenter. He made observations, worked out possible explanations and put them to the test. He was not successful every time, but he was always asking questions and trying to find answers to them by experiment.

■ *For more about the electric motor see pp126–7. For more about transformers see pp130–31.*

THE electric MOTOR

The vacuum cleaner, electric drill, hedge trimmer, food processor, fan oven, microwave oven turntable, electric train, spin-drier, personal stereo, compact disc player, tape deck, record deck, hair-drier, milk float, lawn mower . . . the list goes on. These are just some of the many things that rely on the electric motor to make

them work, and that make our daily life easier and more convenient.

There are several types of electric motor. Most of them produce rotation, although the linear motor produces movement in a straight line. The monorail trains in some theme parks use linear motors.

The basic principle

A magnetic field is produced around a wire carrying a current. This magnetic field produces a force when the wire is in another magnetic field. The other magnetic field could be produced by another wire or a magnet. The force produces motion. This principle can be seen with a simple demonstration.

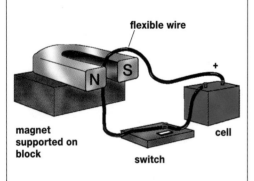

flexible wire

magnet supported on block

cell

switch

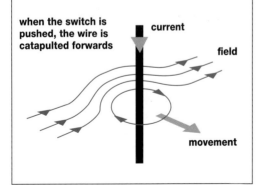

when the switch is pushed, the wire is catapulted forwards

current

field

movement

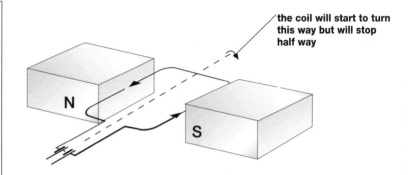

the coil will start to turn this way but will stop half way

N

S

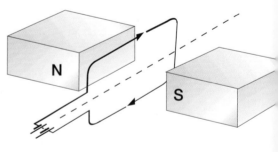

N

S

▲ *If current passes in a coil between two poles the coil will turn through 90°. This is because the magnetism around the wire interacts with the field between the poles of the magnet. However, this coil will not rotate continuously.*

Usually we need a motor that gives continuous movement. This is a matter of design. The simplest type of motor to understand, the **d.c.** (**direct current**) motor, uses a loop of wire between the poles of a magnet.

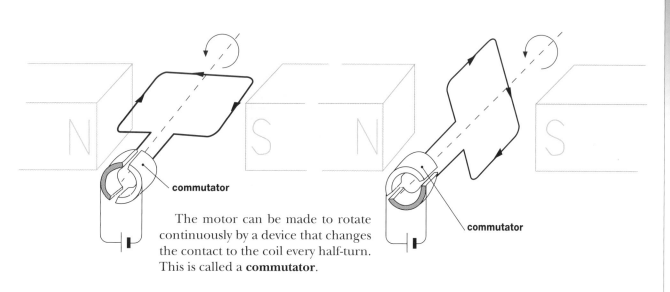

commutator

commutator

The motor can be made to rotate continuously by a device that changes the contact to the coil every half-turn. This is called a **commutator**.

OTHER DESIGNS OF MOTOR

*There are other designs of motor. The **a.c.** motor runs on **alternating current**. A **universal** motor will run on either a.c. or d.c. **Synchronous** a.c. motors run at a constant speed that depends on the frequency of the mains supply. This type of motor was used in electric clocks before cheap quartz clocks were invented. It is also used in some record players.*

A commercial motor has more coils than the simple home-made motor. It also uses an electromagnet in place of an ordinary permanent magnet.

■ *For more about a.c. and d.c. see p130–31.*

▶ *The motor in a vacuum cleaner runs from the alternating current supplied to your house. The motor is used to turn a fan which drives out a powerful stream of air. This sets up a powerful inflowing current of air which carries dust into the vacuum cleaner and is collected in a dust bag or chamber.*

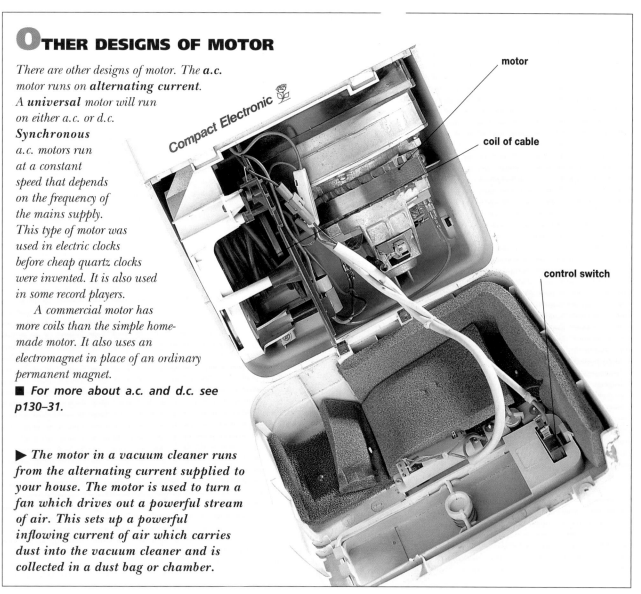

motor

coil of cable

control switch

GENERATING
Electricity

How is electricity made in a power station? If you have a **dynamo** *on your bike then you make electricity when you pedal along. Inside, the dynamo looks something like the diagram on the right.*

▶ *Inside a bicycle dynamo.*

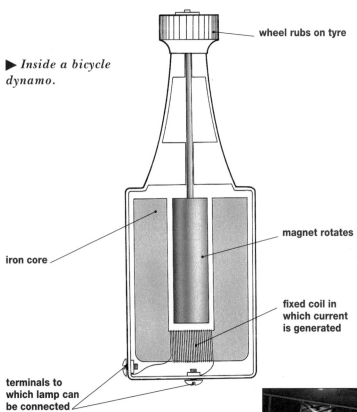

wheel rubs on tyre

magnet rotates

fixed coil in which current is generated

iron core

terminals to which lamp can be connected

When the magnet moves near the coil an electric current flows in the coil. The current transfers energy to the lamps on your bike. Have you noticed what happens to the light when you pedal more slowly when you are using a dynamo? The lights get dimmer. When you stop they go out.

The output from a dynamo can be increased in three ways:

- You can use a coil with more turns;
- You can use a stronger magnet;
- You can increase the speed of rotation by pedalling faster.

G*enerators*

The dynamos in power stations are called **generators**. In a generator, just as in a bike dynamo, a magnet spins inside a coil to produce an electric current. Compared with a bike dynamo, a power station generator is huge – about 70 m long and 6 m across. In thermal power stations water is heated and turned into steam. The heat comes from furnaces fired by coal, gas, or oil or from a nuclear reactor. The energy from the steam is transferred to a turbine which drives the spinning magnet. In hydroelectric power stations the turbines are turned by water falling from a height.

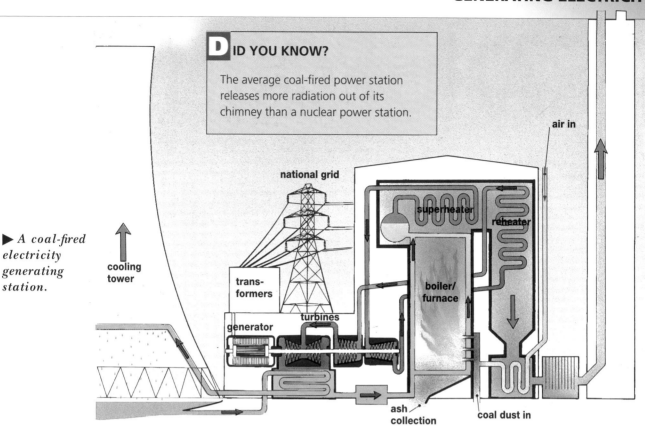

air in

national grid

superheater

reheater

cooling tower

trans-formers

boiler/ furnace

turbines

generator

ash collection

coal dust in

◀ *A coal-fired electricity generating station.*

Power stations

A bicycle dynamo produces electricity at about 5 Js⁻¹. A power station generator may produce electricity at about 500 000 000 Js⁻¹!

A power station transfers only about one-third of the energy of the fuel into electricity. The rest is usually spread out, for example in the warm water poured into rivers or in the steam escaping from the cooling towers into the atmosphere.

Many European power stations make good use of the warm water produced, however. These are called **combined heat and power stations**. These power stations are attached to a pipe network which carries the waste hot water around buildings in the local community and supplies them with heat. In Sweden about 20 per cent of heating is supplied like this, but little is supplied in this way in the United Kingdom.

■ *For more about nuclear power stations see p50–51.*

■ *For more about alternative methods of generating electricity see p46–9.*

◀ *This generator produced up to 350 million watts (MW) of electricity at full speed. It converts the kinetic energy of superheated steam into electricity.*

UNITS OF MEASUREMENT

The number of joules per second produced by power stations is so large that the measurement is usually in megawatts, or even gigawatts.

1 W (watt) = 1 Js⁻¹

1 MW (megawatt) = 1 000 000 Js⁻¹

TRANSFORMERS

A transformer changes the size of a voltage. There are transformers in your television set, computer, radio, door bell, battery charger, stereo system and many other things. Most of the circuits in these appliances run at between 6 V and 30 V. A mains plug provides electricity at 240 V. The transformers in the appliances change the 240 V from the mains to whatever smaller voltages their circuits need.

NATIONAL GRID

Another important use of transformers is in the National Grid, which transmits electricity around the country. Without transformers, most of the electricity produced would be wasted in heating up the overhead power lines. When an electric current flows down wires they warm up. Sometimes we want this to happen – that's how the element of a kettle or an electric blanket works. But warming up overhead power cables would be a waste of energy.

If the current in a power cable is very low and the voltage is very high, the energy can be transferred without heating up the cable very much. So a transformer is used at the start of a power line to increase the voltage. This type of transformer is called a **step up transformer***. At the consumer end of the power line another transformer changes high voltage back to the lower level required. This kind is called a* **step down transformer***.*

DID YOU KNOW?

The electric current produced by a power station generator is alternating current. This is called a.c. for short. The direction of the current flow changes backwards and forwards 50 times every second. The spinning magnet in the generator rotates 50 times a second. How often the current alternates depends on how fast the magnet spins.

The current from a battery flows in a constant direction. This is called direct current or d.c. for short.

■ *For more about a.c. and d.c. see p126–7.*

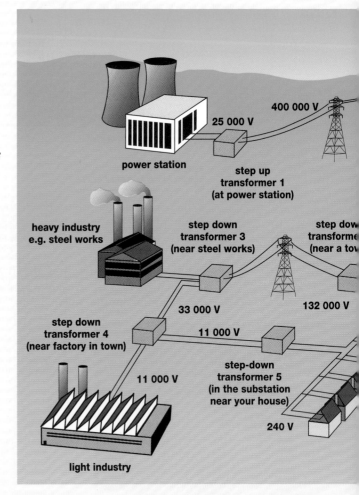

power station

25 000 V

400 000 V

step up transformer 1 (at power station)

heavy industry e.g. steel works

step down transformer 3 (near steel works)

step down transformer (near a tow

33 000 V

132 000 V

11 000 V

step down transformer 4 (near factory in town)

step-down transformer 5 (in the substation near your house)

11 000 V

240 V

light industry

▲ *400 KV is too high a voltage to supply to people's homes. So the voltage is stepped down to 240 V in several stages.*

How a transformer works

A transformer consists of a ring of iron with two coils wrapped on it. Commercial transformers are often wound in more complex ways than the one shown here, to make them more efficient and to give a choice of voltages, but the principle is the same.

Transformers work on a.c. (alternating current). The coil that the current goes

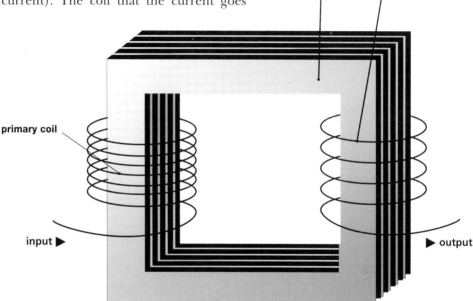

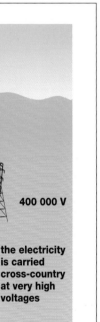

400 000 V

the electricity is carried cross-country at very high voltages

▲ *This is a step down transformer. The secondary coil has fewer turns than the primary coil.*

into is called the **primary coil**. Because the current is changing direction 50 times a second, a changing magnetic field is produced in the iron core. The changing magnetic field induces a voltage in the **secondary coil** (a bit like the moving magnet in Faraday's experiment of 1831).

The size of the voltage produced in the secondary coil is related to the size of the voltage applied to the primary coil. Simply:

The ratio of the voltages is the same as the ratio of the numbers of turns in the coils.

So if the secondary coil has half the turns of the primary, the secondary voltage will be half the voltage in the primary coil. This is a step down transformer. In any step down transformer, the secondary coil has fewer turns than the primary coil. In a step

up transformer, the secondary coil has more turns than the primary coil, and the voltage is increased. This sounds like we are getting something for nothing, but we don't. If the voltage goes up then the current goes down, and vice versa.

Although the transformer is very efficient, it's not perfect. The coils produce heat and the core heats up. (That is part of the reason why the back of a computer gets warm when it is on!) You still have to transfer more energy to a transformer than you get back from the secondary circuit. You can never gain energy. It's just a matter of transferring it in a more convenient form to use.

■ *For more about Faraday's experiments see p124–5.*

MATERIALS

All the things we use everyday have come, either directly or indirectly, from the Earth's atmosphere or from its crust. The Earth contains the **raw materials** for making useful **products**. Some raw materials that make important contributions to our lifestyle, which come from the Earth's crust include oil, coal, metal ores, salts, limestone and sulphur. We use oxygen and nitrogen from the atmosphere. Wood and wool, for example, come from living things on Earth.

Minerals

The Earth, and all the living things upon it and in it, is made up of only about 90 elements. Sometimes the elements are found free, that is they are uncombined with other elements. For example, yellow crystals of free sulphur are sometimes found, so too are free gold, silver and diamond (one of the crystalline forms of the element carbon). But this is rare; most elements are found in combination with other elements. These combinations are known as **chemical compounds**. Naturally occurring compounds found in the Earth's crust are often called **minerals**.

▶ *Diamonds occur as octahedral rounded structures. Because of their hardness they are used for cutting and drilling equipment.*

Diamond

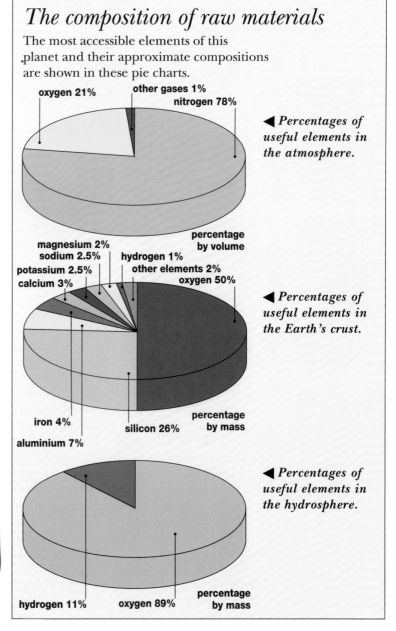

The composition of raw materials

The most accessible elements of this planet and their approximate compositions are shown in these pie charts.

oxygen 21%   other gases 1%
nitrogen 78%

◀ *Percentages of useful elements in the atmosphere.*

percentage by volume

magnesium 2%
sodium 2.5%
potassium 2.5%
calcium 3%
hydrogen 1%
other elements 2%
oxygen 50%

◀ *Percentages of useful elements in the Earth's crust.*

iron 4%
aluminium 7%
silicon 26%

percentage by mass

◀ *Percentages of useful elements in the hydrosphere.*

hydrogen 11%   oxygen 89%   percentage by mass

Some minerals are found in an almost pure state. Limestone, for example, is almost pure calcium carbonate. Other minerals are found in rocks as mixtures. Granite contains crystals of three important minerals: quartz, feldspar and biotile mica. Metal **ores** are rocks that contain minerals from which a metal or other useful substance can be extracted.

■ *For more about elements see pp96–7.*

Gold

▲ *Crystals of gold on a sample of quarz.*

Cinnabar

◀ *Cinnabar is mercury sulphide. It is the most important ore of mercury.*

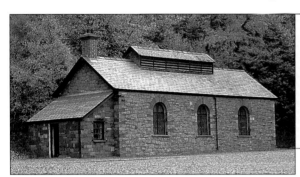

Slate
Useful properties - Can be split into flat sheets.
Uses - As a roofing material.

◀ *A slate roof.*

Granite
Useful properties - Plentiful, very hard, attractive, especially when polished.
Uses - Building and ornamental stone.

Gravestone made from polished granite. ▶

Sandstone
Useful properties - Plentiful, abrasive, can be moderately hard, but often crumbles to sand.
Uses - Building stone. Sand has many uses, including as an abrasive and for making glass.

◀ *Remains of sandstone columns.*

Limestone
Useful properties - Plentiful, often quite hard (but reacts with acid) attractive colour, source of calcium carbonate.
Uses - Building.

Limestone was used to build this house. ▶

Marble
Useful properties - Hard (but it reacts with acid), is very attractive.
Uses - As a decorative stone for buildings, sculptures, etc.

◀ *This statue is made from marble.*

Pure Materials

The word 'pure' is often used in conversation. It has many meanings. It can mean 'spotless', 'blameless' or 'innocent', or it can mean 'free from unwanted materials'. The word appears on many labels advertising everyday products.

To a scientist these materials are not pure. So why is the word 'pure' added to their names? 'Pure new wool' contains woollen fibres and nothing else. 'Pure brilliant white' means that the paint is a spotless white. Can you think why 'pure' is used in the names of other materials?

In science, **pure material** has a special meaning. A pure material contains only one substance. A material that is made up of two or more different substances is called a **mixture**. Mixtures are far more common than pure materials. There are five main kinds of mixture:

Separating Mixtures

Nearly all natural materials are mixtures. Mixtures often have to be separated into pure materials. The method chosen to obtain pure materials from a mixture depends upon the type of mixture.

Here is a pure substance you might use or handle today. ▶

mercury thermometer   **copper wire**

Each of these materials had to be separated from other substances before you could use it! Can you find out what methods were used for each one? ◀

And here are some everyday

Type of mixture

Solid-Solid	Solid-Liquid	Liquid-Liquid	Liquid-Gas	Gas-Gas
ROCK e.g. GRANITE	ANT-ACID MEDICINE	SALAD DRESSING	FIZZY LEMONADE	AIR

and Mixtures

Q Why is it important to know if a material is pure?

A In industry, manufacturers need to know exactly what the starting materials are. Impurities in an ingredient could affect the finished product. For example, impurities in the slip clay used to make hand·basins and toilets can produce holes in the pottery when it is fired in the kiln, making it useless. Can you think of any other possible reasons?

Q How do scientists decide if a material is pure?

A Here are some important ways of finding out:
- observation
- measuring temperature against time with respect to melting and boiling
- chromatography

Q How does observation help?

A Sometimes you can see that a material contains more than one substance.

Q How can the temperature at which something melts or boils help?

A Finding out what happens to the temperature of a material when it is heated to make it melt or boil can tell us clearly whether it is pure or a mixture of substances. If it is a pure substance it will have a fixed melting or boiling point. If it is a mixture it will melt or boil over a range of temperatures.

Q How can chromatography help?

A This is how chromatography is used to show if a material is pure or a mixture.

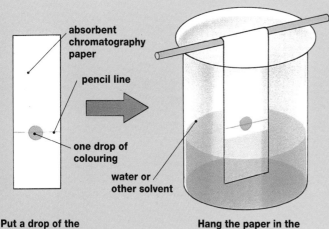

absorbent chromatography paper

pencil line

one drop of colouring

water or other solvent

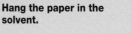

separated dyes

leave for a few minutes

Put a drop of the colouring on to chromatography paper.

Hang the paper in the solvent.

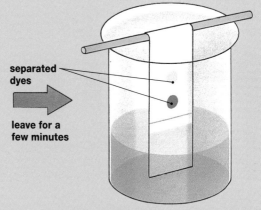

Water rises up the paper, separating the dyes in the colouring. In this case, the yellow prefers the solvent, so it travels further. The blue prefers to stick to the paper.

Materials IN THE □□□□□□ HOME

There are many different materials used to build a house. The architect Le Corbusier said that a house was 'a machine for living in'. It is easy to forget how complicated a modern house design can be, because most of it is hidden away behind wallpaper, paint and carpets.

A house is a structure designed so that the people inside it can live comfortably despite the changing weather and conditions of daylight outside. We tend to take it for granted, but apart from warmth when and where we want it we also need the inside of a house to be dry and have access to water and electricity. We must be able to get rid of waste materials from cooking, heating and even from our own bodies easily, healthily and quietly.

Choice of materials

The choice of materials for building houses has gradually developed over many years. New materials are constantly being found to improve things. For instance, during the last 20 years there has been a big change from wooden to plastic window frames in many houses, particularly with the increase in the number of homes which have double glazing installed.

The choice of materials in house construction is usually based on a combination of factors such as:

- ease of use
- availability
- cost
- strength
- density
- durability
- safety (e.g. fire resistance)

Some common building materials and their properties are described below.

BRICKS

There are several different types of brick, but they are usually made from clay. Bricks are able to withstand large **compressive forces** (forces that crush them) – a common brick has a compressive strength of between 35 and 50 MNm^{-2}. This means that a single common brick can support more than 30 000 bricks without being crushed!

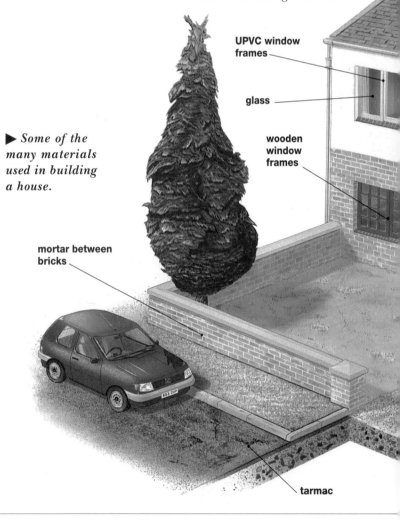

▶ *Some of the many materials used in building a house.*

UPVC window frames

glass

wooden window frames

mortar between bricks

tarmac

PLASTERBOARD

Plasterboard is a **composite** material. It is made from gypsum plaster faced on both sides with heavy paper. Plaster on its own is a brittle material that cracks easily; paper is made from fibres which have some **tensile strength**. The combined material can be handled in sheets and nailed up on wooden beams to give large flat areas, which can be quickly skimmed with plaster

Internal walls that do not need to support the weight of the building above that can be made from a framework of wooden joists covered with plasterboard. This is then skimmed with plaster, and is sometimes called a **stud partition** wall.

PLASTIC

Plastic is now used in many areas of house construction replacing the more traditional materials. Gutters can be made from cast iron or other metals or wood. Plastic is replacing these materials; it is cheaper, lighter weight, and does not need painting or maintaining because it does not rot. Plastic is also used in doors and window frames for the same reasons. The plastic is moulded around aluminium sections which are light but give the plastic additional strength. One drawback is the limited range of colours which is available.

WOOD

There are many different types of timber used in building. Floor sections are often made from chipboard, which is a composite material made from wood chips bonded together with **resin**. Chipboard has the advantage over standard floorboards that it is not attacked by woodworm, and does not have to be treated to prevent it from being attacked by fungus.

However, the main enemy of wood is damp, the microscopic spores of the **dry rot** fungus drift everywhere but they will germinate only when the moisture content is above 20 per cent. Houses are designed to keep the damp out so that the moisture content does not get high enough for dry rot to set in. This is achieved with air bricks set in the walls, gutters to carry away rainwater, pointing between bricks, the damp proof course and lead flashing where the chimney meets the roof.

CEMENT, MORTAR AND CONCRETE

Cement is made by roasting clay and limestone together and grinding the mixture to a powder. If water is added to the powder and it dries, the cement sets hard. **Mortar** is a mixture of cement, sand and water which is used to stick building bricks and blocks together. **Concrete** is a mixture of cement, sand, gravel and water that sets to a hard rock-type solid, which is very good at resisting compressive forces. It is used in houses for foundations and some floors.

■ *For more about materials see p132–5.*

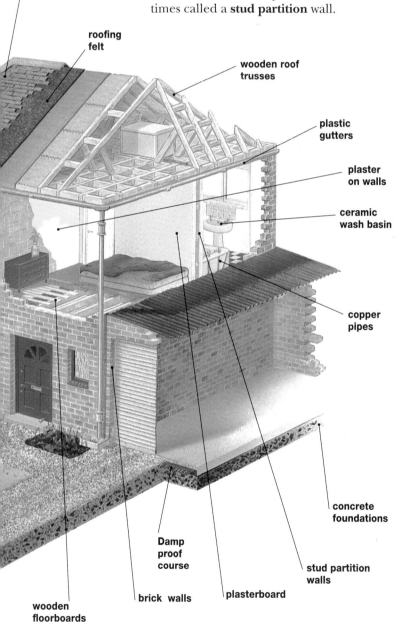

slates

roofing felt

wooden roof trusses

plastic gutters

plaster on walls

ceramic wash basin

copper pipes

concrete foundations

Damp proof course

stud partition walls

brick walls

plasterboard

wooden floorboards

PESTICIDES AN

Chemicals used in farming are called **agrochemicals**. *The agrochemicals that are used to kill pests are called* **pesticides**. *These are of three main types:* **Fungicides** *(chemicals that kill fungi),* **insecticides** *(chemicals that kill insects) and* **herbicides** *(chemicals that kill plants).*

To improve the production of crops chemicals are used which prevent infection by fungal diseases or attack from insects or smothering by weeds. One reason why food is plentiful and cheap in the western world (Europe and North America) is because these chemicals are used.

Problems with pesticides

Using a chemical to kill, say, an insect pest might solve one pest problem, but it can cause others. For example, the chemical might kill other insects as well as the pests. Insects like ladybirds and bees are useful: some eat pests, others help in fertilising plants. Sometimes when one pest is killed off, a more destructive pest takes its place.

Herbicides

Herbicides are useful because they can kill weeds which compete with food crops. The weeds compete for water, minerals, light and space; if they are allowed to grow freely, the yield from the food crop can be severely reduced. Many herbicides are known as **selective herbicides** – this means that they kill the weeds but not the food crop, so that they can be sprayed on to the whole field. However, they may also kill wild plants growing along the edges of the field. Herbicides may also affect many of the insects and other small animals living in and around the field.

DDT AND DIELDRIN

DDT and dieldrin are powerful insecticides. Lots of farmers used them in the 1940s and 1950s. Gradually people began to realise that these chemicals were having unexpected effects on wildlife. For example, the graph shows how the population of peregrine falcons in the United Kingdom has changed over the last 60 years.

Peregrine populations

The use of DDT and dieldrin was restricted in the years 1962 to 1976. Following this, the population of peregrine falcons began to rise.

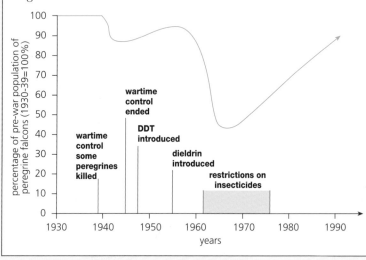

It was discovered that the insecticides had entered the falcons' food chain. The chemicals were getting into the birds' bodies and poisoning them. One effect was that the falcons laid eggs with very thin shells, which were easily broken in the nest so few of them hatched.

None of this had been realised when DDT and dieldrin were first used. Now their use is banned in countries all over the world.

INSECTICIDES

What do we do now?

▲ If DDT is sprayed on the plant, traces of it will pass up the food chain which may result in the animals at the top of the chain being poisoned. Humans may eat contaminated crops or animals that have fed on them.

DDT and dieldrin remain in the environment for years and years. It has been calculated that every living thing on Earth now contains traces of DDT! However, newer agrochemicals are safer to use. Many of them disintegrate after they have done their job. For example, the insecticide **permethrin** breaks down when it is exposed to light. It can be used to protect a whole range of crops, including apples and cereals in Europe and cotton in the tropics.

Permethrin is very similar to a natural insecticide found in some plants. Scientists are developing other methods of pest control – for example, using bacteria to kill insect pests. Some farmers grow food without using any pesticides at all! There are several reasons why some people prefer to use fewer chemicals:

● many chemicals are expensive
● chemicals can damage the micro-organisms in the soil
● chemicals can contaminate water running off the fields
● chemicals can cause risks to human and animal life

■ *For more about using bacteria for pest control see p140–41.*

A natural

▲ *Black bean aphids are infesting this bean plant.*

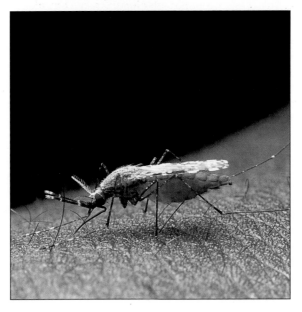

▶ *When a mosquito punctures the skin to suck blood it may pass on malaria.*

Insects are among the most serious pests of food crops that we know. They are also responsible for carrying certain diseases, some of which are fatal to humans.

Huge amounts of money have been spent developing insecticides. Recently new types of insecticide have been developed which do not have the disadvantages of chemicals like DDT. They are called **biological** or **'natural' insecticides** because they are based on living organisms and the chemicals they produce. Microorganisms are usually used as they are the natural enemies of insect pests.

INSECTICIDE

▲ *The life cycle of the cabbage white butterfly. Eggs are hatched on the cabbage leaves and these develop into caterpillars which feed on the leaves. The caterpillar then metamorphosises into a butterfly.*

A common garden pest is the cabbage white butterfly. When members of the cabbage family such as sprouts and broccoli are grown in very large numbers in market gardens, for example, the cabbage white is a serious economic pest because it will eat the plant leaves.

BIOLOGICAL INSECTICIDE

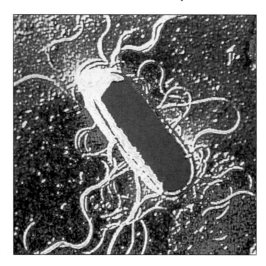

Nature's friend is among the wide variety of insecticide sprays which you can buy in some garden centres. This spray is different from chemical insecticides. It contains living microorganisms which will grow and multiply if they are given food and water, for example on growth jelly. They can be seen only using a microscope. One such microorganism is a bacterium called *Bacillus thuringiensis.*

When you want to treat cabbages you can mix up some of the insecticide powder in cold water and spray it on the plants. The caterpillars take in some of the spray as they munch their way through the cabbage leaves. Within an hour or so they become paralysed due to the action of a poison that the bacteria produce. After about a day, the caterpillars die and fall off the cabbages. However, the microorganisms used are harmless to humans.

Insecticides like *Nature's friend* have proved so effective that they have been used all over the world against insect pests. For example, they are used in the United States on a large scale for spraying crops and forests. The deliberate use by humans of one living organism in order to kill another (a pest) is called **biological pest control**.

■ *For more about insecticides see p38–9.*
■ *For more about bacteria see p144–7.*

◄ **Bacillus thuringiensis** *causes damage to insect larvae but is harmless to humans and other animals.*

Drugs and

What is a drug?

A drug is a chemical substance that can affect the working of the body. People have been using certain drugs for thousands of years, usually as medicines to treat diseases and illness.

One such drug is opium. Opium comes from a kind of poppy and is a very strong **sedative** (it makes the patient drowsy). It is also a powerful painkiller. But opium has a very serious **side-effect** (this means an extra effect, often an unpleasant one). It is **addictive** – people may end up taking the drug because they feel they can't do without it.

The reason why heroin and crack are so dangerous is that they are addictive. In fact, heroin is a very pure form of opium.

Most medicines contain drugs but not all drugs are medicines

Cough mixtures and 'flu medicines contain drugs to treat cough or 'flu symptoms. Their labels tell you which drugs they contain. For example, a cough linctus might contain extract of ipecacuanha, which is a type of cactus that contains a drug. A common 'flu remedy contains the drug paracetamol, which reduces fever and eases headaches.

Whisky contains alcohol, and cigarettes contain nicotine. Alcohol and nicotine are drugs. But whisky and cigarettes are not medicines: alcohol and nicotine are harmful to the body.

Plants containing useful drugs

Plant	Drug	Use
foxglove	digitalis	treatment of heart conditions
opium poppy	opium (morphine)	painkiller/ sedative
willow	aspirin-like drug	painkiller
coca	cocaine	painkiller/ mood-altering drug
deadly nightshade	atropine	affects the heart
cinchona tree	quinine	treatment of malaria

▲ *Digitalis is used as a heart stimulant. It is extracted from the foxglove.*

Medicines

Where do drugs come from?

PLANTS

At one time, almost all the drugs in use were extracted directly from plants. Some of the plants in your garden may contain essential medical drugs. For example, foxgloves contain an important drug called digitalis. South American Indians used the leaves of the coca plant as a medicine. This plant contains the chemical cocaine. Cocaine and chemicals like it are important painkillers and have been prescribed by doctors and dentists for many years. But cocaine, too, can be highly addictive.

MOULDS

Some important and powerful chemicals are produced by moulds (fungi). These are called **antibiotics**. They include penicillin, streptomycin and tetracycline. Antibiotics are used to treat bacterial infections. You have probably been given antibiotics if you have ever been ill with tonsillitis, ear-ache or bronchitis.

▶ *Quinine is used to prevent malaria. It is extracted from Cinchona tree.*

SYNTHETIC DRUGS

In 1909 the first **synthetic** (artificial) drug was made. A team of German scientists led by Paul Ehrlich was trying to find a chemical that could be used to treat an unpleasant sexually transmitted disease called syphilis. Now it is treated with antibiotics, but at the beginning of the century there was no treatment: in Germany it accounted for 6 per cent of deaths, and in France it accounted for 10 per cent. Four out of every five people who developed the disease died.

The 606th chemical made by Ehrlich's team (they called it just '606' but later it was called **salvarsan**) was tested on some people who had syphilis – and it worked! Nearly all of them were cured.

Unfortunately, no-one knew how much (the dose) of the drug to give. As with any drug, too little had no effect, yet too much caused side-effects. One side-effect of the drug was deafness. However, after tests, salvarsan, the first synthetic drug, was put on the market. Ehrlich called it a 'magic bullet', because it targeted the bacteria causing the disease and killed them – no-one knew how or why, but it worked.

Later many other synthetic drugs were made. One important group was the **sulpha drugs**, developed in the 1920s. These were successful in treating a whole range of infections and diseases, including pneumonia and septicaemia (blood poisoning).

■ *For more about antibiotics see p152–3.*

▼ *Deadly nightshade is poisonous. However, the drug atropine is extracted from it and this is used to treat the heart.*

BACTERIA

Bacteria

Since the invention of the microscope in the 1600s, scientists have been able to see cells. Plant and animal cells were the first types of cell to be seen. For a long time a whole group of cells, bacteria, went unnoticed, mainly because they were very small.

A number of scientists in the 1800s made some very important discoveries about bacteria and started the battle against diseases.

The 'Sherlock Holmes' of disease

Louis Pasteur and Robert Koch were brilliant investigators who proved that tiny bacteria caused some of the dreadful diseases which affected humans and animals. Many scientists in the 1850s did not believe that bacteria existed, let alone that they could cause diseases!

Pasteur demonstrated that those tiny cells (or 'germs' as they were then called) caused food to go 'off'. He also proved that certain bacteria caused diseases in moths and cows as well as in people. Koch identified many different bacteria. He showed that the bacteria which caused gangrene was different from the one which caused abscesses.

Joseph Lister (1827–1912) was a British surgeon who changed surgical practice with the introduction of antiseptics. Lister's antiseptic solution of carbolic acid was used to clean wounds and to scrub surgeons' hands. This reduced the risk of bacterial infection during surgery. Previously antiseptics like tar and mercury had been used to kill bacteria. However, these often harmed the patients. Lister also devised new operations and invented several surgical instruments.

In England at about the same time a young doctor called Joseph Lister had improved the chances of survival following operations by using **antiseptic** chemicals (antiseptic means against septicaemia). Many doctors at that time did not realise

---

Each of the following diseases is caused by a different bacterium.

Anthrax A disease which affects cattle and humans, the bacteria accumulate in the blood of the infected individual and may turn the blood black!

Diphtheria A disease which infects the nasal passages; the bacteria produce a poison which may damage many other organs in the body.

Tuberculosis A disease which often causes terrible coughing fits. The bacteria sometimes invade part of the lung.

Venereal diseases These diseases are sexually transmitted. That means the disease is passed from one person to another during sexual intercourse.

Sometimes the bacteria look different from one another but sometimes they appear very similar and can be recognised only by chemical tests or the different way they stain with dyes.

and VIRUSES

that the antiseptic works because the chemical kills the bacteria. After the work of Pasteur and Koch it was realised how important bacteria are in causing diseases.

How the body defends itself

By the 1800s the 'germ theory' was accepted. The idea that diseases could be caused by bacteria or germs meant that the scientists could do something about curing these diseases. In 1882 a Russian scientist called Metchnikoff made a very important discovery.

Using a microscope he watched certain cells inside a jellyfish. He noticed that these cells moved around, and when Metchnikoff put a tiny wooden splinter into the jellyfish these cells seemed to attack the point of the splinter. Metchnikoff suggested that in the human body there were special cells which attacked any intruder, like bacteria, which get into the body. We now know that there are such cells in the bloodstream; they are called **phagocytes** or white blood cells.

Immunity

Pasteur and Koch both invented ways of treating, and often curing, dangerous diseases. The methods they used sometimes involved injecting the patient with weakened bacteria. After the injection, the white blood cells in the bloodstream multiply and then attack the bacterial cells. Because the bacteria are weakened, or may even be dead, the white blood cells can overcome them. The body defences are then prepared in case of a new invasion by the fully active bacteria – the body has developed immunity to this particular bacterium and its disease. This treatment is called **immunisation**.

You may have had a BCG-tuberculin test at school. A small holder with six small needles is scratched on to your arm. If the scratch swells up, this shows that you have some immunity to tuberculosis. If there is no swelling you may need an injection to make sure that you develop immunity to this dangerous bacterium.

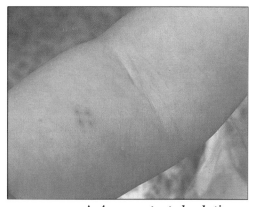

▲ *A concentrated solution of tuberculin is applied to the skin using a special needled device. The reaction is then read 3 to 10 days later. Individuals showing little or no reactivity to the tuberculin (as here) have not developed an immunity to the disease and are then vaccinated with BCG. BCG stands for Bacille Calmette Guerin after the two Frenchmen who developed the vaccine in 1906.*

Robert Koch (1843–1910) was a German doctor who founded the study of bacteria. He identified the bacteria that cause diseases such as cholera, tuberculosis and anthrax. He also studied malaria and concluded that it is caused by mosquito bites, at the same time as the British doctor Ronald Ross. Koch received the 1905 Nobel Prize in medicine.

BACTERIA

It is now known that there are different types of white blood cells. Some cells, called phagocytes, actually attack bacteria and engulf them. Other white blood cells called **lymphocytes** *make chemicals called* **antibodies** *which make the bacteria cells stick together so that the phagocytes can engulf the bacteria more easily.*

Viruses

The first step in finding a cure for a disease is to find the bacterium that causes the disease. However, certain diseases which were studied seemed to have no bacteria linked with them. This proved to be quite a puzzle for a long time. Pasteur had this trouble when he tried to find a cure for rabies.

By 1890 many scientists suspected that there were other tiny living things which caused certain diseases because no bacterial cells could be found, even when the best microscopes were used.

By 1915 these tiny organisms had been given the name **virus** (the word means a living poisonous liquid). This is because they could be extracted in a liquid form which could cause a disease, although they could not be seen in the liquid. It was also realised at this time that *any* type of cell could be attacked by a virus: plant cells, animal cells, human cells and even bacterial cells could be attacked.

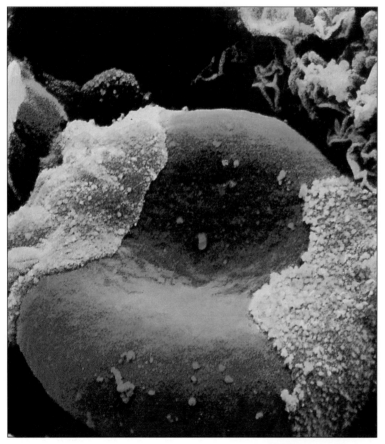

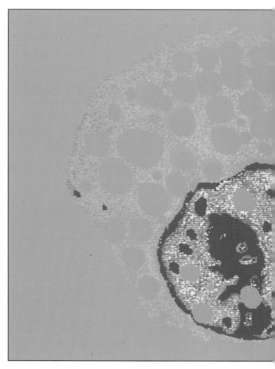

Each different type of invading bacterium causes a different antibody to be made. Once this has happened, the person is said to be immunised against that particular type of bacterium and the disease it may cause. Antibodies can stay in the bloodstream for years and so protect the person from future invasions by particular bacteria.

▲ *Phagocytic white cells (white/yellow) engulf foreign bodies including bacteria and, in this case, an old red blood cell.*

and VIRUSES

Viruses were not actually seen until the 1950s. This was because scientists needed a very powerful microscope to see them. The first **electron microscope** was designed and built in 1940. Once this electron microscope was available, scientists were able to see a whole range of viruses – some of them cause the worst diseases known.

*L*ouis Pasteur (1822–95) was a French chemist and biologist. He invented the process for killing bacteria in milk, called pasteurisation. In 1881 he developed a vaccine against the disease anthrax in sheep and later a vaccine against rabies in humans.

■ *For more about diseases see p148–155.*

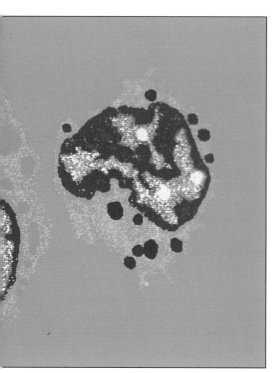

Diseases caused by viruses

Poliomyelitis This virus causes polio. Polio used to be quite common before 1950 in the United Kingdom. It often affected the legs of children, causing twisting. It is still a problem in many countries.

Measles This is a common infectious disease in children. In some countries measles causes many infant deaths each year.

Smallpox This is a terrible disease which can cause disfigurement and death. Smallpox was very common throughout the world, but recently the World Health Organisation had a massive immunisation programme and has managed to **eradicate** the disease.

Influenza Many people each year die of influenza. After the First World War, in the 1920s, there was a **pandemic** (worldwide epidemic) of influenza during which millions of people died.

Rabies A terrible disease usually found in animals but sometimes caught by humans. Rabies causes madness and is usually fatal. The only treatment was devised by Louis Pasteur.

◄ *This T-lymphocyte (left) has just given the 'kiss of death' to its target cell (right). The lymphocyte releases enzymes that disrupt the target cell's membrane to destroy the cell.*

Vaccines

The main treatments for disease-causing viruses are to inject or take **orally** (by mouth) a **serum** or a small weak dose of the disease so that the body can develop immunity to the virus. One example which you may have come across is the sugar lump containing a tiny drop of weakened polio virus. Such liquids which cause immunity to build up in a person are called **vaccines.**

NEW

A strange feature of bacteria and viruses is that they change from time to time. Just when we think we've got a disease cured, the bacterium or virus changes, or mutates. Sometimes a completely new disease appears which we have never seen before.

This is often when a bacterium or virus changes completely and becomes very dangerous. Sometimes, however, a new disease appears, not because the bacterium or virus has changed but because the circumstances of our daily lives have changed.

Influenza

Why do people suffer from 'flu year after year? This is because although you have immunity to the 'flu you suffered from last year, the new 'flu which arrives the following year, or later, may be slightly different. The virus has changed. This means that last year's immunity won't work on the new virus!

Legionnaires Disease

In 1976 a group of ex-servicemen in Philadelphia, in the United States, were at a big meeting in one of the city's largest hotels. Rather mysteriously, a number of them died. At first the doctors suspected a severe form of food poisoning. But the symptoms were not typical of food poisoning and many other people had eaten the same food and were perfectly fine. The doctors and scientists of the public health services had a mystery on their hands.

In 1979, a scientist working at a special laboratory which studies diseases, in Georgia found a bacterium in tissues taken from the dead men. This bacterium proved to be the cause of a new disease which is now called Legionnaires Disease (because the ex-servicemen were Legionnaires).

Since then, it has been discovered that the bacterium lives and grows in water, especially in heating systems or large storage tanks which have not been chlorinated. If the bacterium infects a person it causes a type of pneumonia.

This disease is probably not a *new* disease; doctors may have mistaken it for pneumonia in the past. What is new is the modern lifestyle which has provided this bacterium with places to grow in close contact with older people who may have lower resistance to the disease it causes.

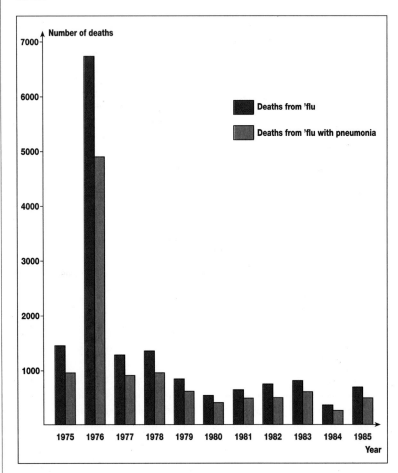

◀ *This graph shows the number of deaths from influenza in England and Wales. Vaccination against influenza is difficult because the virus develops different strains.*

DISEASES

AIDS

Probably the most notorious new disease is AIDS (**A**cquired **I**mmune **D**eficiency **S**yndrome). No-one is sure exactly where it came from, but it has spread very quickly. It is a sexually transmitted disease: that means it can be passed from person to person during sexual intercourse. It can also be passed on if blood from an AIDS sufferer comes into contact with a healthy person, such as through a cut or scratch, or by drug addicts who share needles or syringes.

The reason it is so dangerous is that it attacks the body's defence or **immune system**. It is thought that the agent causing AIDS is a virus, the **HIV virus**. This can stop the body's natural defences working, having a disastrous effect on the health of the person. Every bacterium or virus that comes into contact with AIDS sufferers can infect them: they are defenceless to protect themselves.

The virus invades one type of cell called a T_4 **Helper Cell**. This cell is a lymphocyte cell (a type of white blood cell) and it controls most of the other cells involved with attacking bacteria or virus cells. For example, the T_4 cell controls the cells which produce antibodies. If the T_4 cells are damaged or destroyed then the body's whole antibody production is prevented or reduced. This is what eventually causes the death of the majority of AIDS sufferers. It isn't the AIDS virus which kills the person, it is the secondary infections, such as pneumonia, which they cannot fight off.

A peculiar aspect of the AIDS infection is that it can lie dormant for years. The sufferer may know that he/she is carrying the virus but doesn't actually feel ill at all. Many scientists and doctors are working hard to discover treatments for this disease. Unfortunately no complete cure is known as yet.

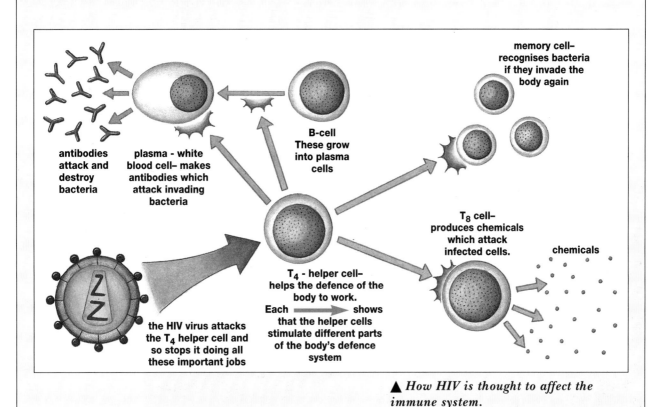

memory cell– recognises bacteria if they invade the body again

antibodies attack and destroy bacteria

plasma - white blood cell– makes antibodies which attack invading bacteria

B-cell These grow into plasma cells

T_8 cell– produces chemicals which attack infected cells.

chemicals

T_4 - helper cell– helps the defence of the body to work. Each ➡ shows that the helper cells stimulate different parts of the body's defence system

the HIV virus attacks the T_4 helper cell and so stops it doing all these important jobs

▲ *How HIV is thought to affect the immune system.*

NEW

Helping the body to defend itself

The body has its own defence system which is very efficient. The most important part of the body's defences are the white blood cells. There are a number of different types of white blood cell, some engulf ('eat') bacteria. These are sometimes called phagocytes (pronounced fadge-o-sites).

Other white blood cells produce special chemicals called antibodies. These antibodies stick to foreign cells like bacterial cells. This tends to stop the bacterial cell functioning properly. It also makes it easier for the phagocytes to engulf the bacteria.

For each different type of bacteria which might get inside the body, the defence system will produce different antibodies.

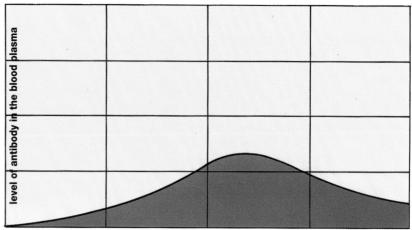

1 First infection

a type of microorganism enters the body for the first time

white blood cells capture the microorganism

information about microorganism passed to another white blood cell

white blood cells make antibodies

antibodies released

as the reaction is slow, some microorganisms may cause disease

antibody traps microorganisms and makes them clump together

microorganisms eaten by white blood cells

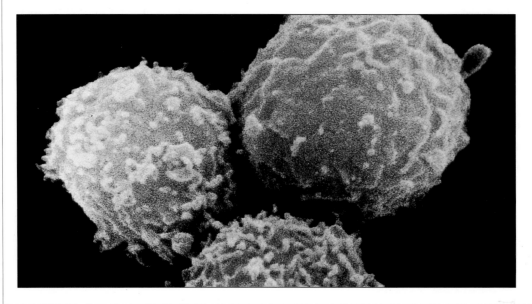

▲ The body's immune system reacts much quicker when a microorganism reinvades.

◄ These white blood cells have antibodies in their surface membranes. The antibodies recognise the invading microorganism.

DISEASES

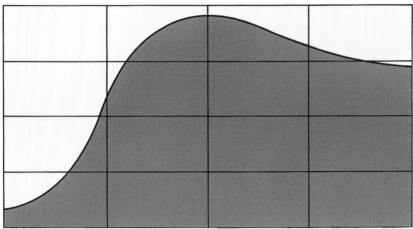

2 Re-infection

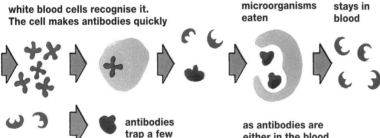

**white blood cells recognise it.
The cell makes antibodies quickly**

**microorganisms
eaten**

**antibody
stays in
blood**

**the same
type of
micro-
organism
enters the
body for the
second time**

**some
antibodies
already in
blood**

**antibodies
trap a few
microorganisms**

**as antibodies are
either in the blood
or made quickly,
the microorganisms
do not damage the
cells - the person is
immune**

IMMUNISATION

Sometimes the body can take a while to produce the correct antibody. When this happens there may be a race between the defences of the body and the speed with which the bacteria reproduce or produce poisons which kill the body's cells. If the number of antibodies is low then there is a danger that the person may become very ill or even die. Their defences lose the battle with the bacteria. In the 18th century, a method of helping the body's defences was discovered. If a person is given a very small dose of a bacteria or virus which would normally cause a disease, the body can build up antibodies to that bacteria or virus. If the body then becomes infected with that same bacteria or virus again, the body's defences are ready and the infecting cells are destroyed. This is called immunisation, because our defence system is called our immune system. Often children are immunised against various disease-causing cells so that they can fight off infections like polio, measles and whooping cough. If you travel to some countries it is wise to have injections so that you are immunised against diseases which are more common in those countries, such as hepatitis and cholera. In school you may well have had test jabs to see if you were immune to TB (tuberculosis). This was a very serious disease early in the 20th century and many people died quite young. The bacteria infects the lungs and gradually destroys the tiny air sacs. If the test jab does not swell up, you need a booster jab. The booster jab stimulates your body to produce lots of antibodies to the TB bacteria.

■ *For more about TB see pp144–5.*

M*edicines*

Antibiotics are some of the best known and most useful medicines because they kill bacteria or stop them multiplying. More importantly they don't harm the person (or animal) they are used in.

■ *For more about medicines see pp142–3.*

ANTIBIOTICS

You may have seen blue or green **moulds** *growing on stale food, damp walls, dead leaves – even on leather. Moulds are* **fungi,** *related to mushrooms and toadstools. They are made up of thread-like cells. When the mould has grown large enough to see, it often looks like a mass of fine cotton wool. This mass of cells is called a* **colony.** *Eventually moulds break down the material they grow on as they use it for food. Moulds spread by producing millions of tiny spores, which are carried around in the air. The spores will grow on anything that contains food.*

Penicillin

In 1928 a scientist called Alexander Fleming was looking at some bacteria he had been growing in a hospital laboratory in London. These were the bacteria that can cause boils and general infections. At that time they often caused serious infections after operations. Fleming noticed something unusual on one of the plates of growth jelly he was using. Something had gone wrong: a mould colony was growing among the bacteria. A mould spore from the air must have landed on the plate. The picture below shows what he saw.

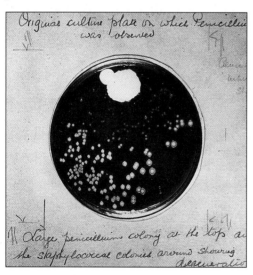

Fleming realised that the mould was producing a chemical which actually stopped bacteria from growing. He tested it to see whether this chemical that destroyed bacteria on a growth jelly could do the same inside a human body.

▶ *Mould growth on a slice of bread after two days (centre) and four days (bottom).*

DID YOU KNOW?

Lots of moulds and other micro-organisms produce chemicals that kill bacteria without harming most animals and humans. These chemicals are called **antibiotics**.

◀ *This is the original culture plate on which penicillin was observed by Fleming in 1929. The large white area is the penicillin, the bacteria around it are being destroyed.*

*A*lexander Fleming (1881–1955) was the British bacteriologist who discovered the life-saving antibiotic penicillin. Fleming worked with Howard Florey and Ernst Chain to extract the antibiotic chemical penicillin from the Penicillium fungus.

MASS PRODUCTION OF ANTIBIOTICS

In the Second World War there was a huge demand for penicillin. War wounds are easily infected by bacteria and many people died from these infections. Giving wounded people penicillin helped them to recover. But in 1940 only tiny amounts of penicillin were available. A tremendous amount of work was done to find a way of producing the drug on a large scale.

Mass production brought down the cost of penicillin dramatically. In 1943, 5 g of penicillin cost about £9000. Now, a course of penicillin tablets can cost the National Health Service less than £1.

The commercial production of antibiotics is big business these days. In the United States in 1990, sales of penicillin were over $400 million!

Antibiotics are made on a vast scale in huge industrial fermentation tanks containing thousands of litres of liquid in which mould is growing. They are like massive brewing vats, except the end result is not beer but penicillin!

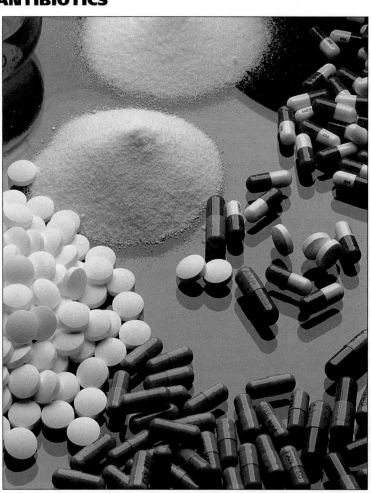

▶ **Antibiotics are available in three forms: tablets, capsules and syrups. Antibiotic syrups tend to be the lowest dosage form and are used to treat children.**

Problems with antibiotics

Because antibiotics are so useful, people everywhere take them – for minor infections as well as for serious ones. Unfortunately, however, bacteria can become resistant to antibiotics especially if an antibiotic is used too much. Once a bacterium becomes resistant to a particular antibiotic then that antibiotic can no longer be used to fight that infection.

So antibiotics work best where they are used only when they are really needed. In Britain you can get antibiotics only on a doctor's prescription, but in many parts of the world they are sold without any special controls. Because of increasing problems of resistance in bacteria, there is a constant search for new antibiotics.

■ **For more about drugs see pp142–3.**
■ **For more about fermentation see p36.**

DISEASE DETEC

*Most diseases have been around for a very long time, but not all of them. There is a new one called **Lyme disease**.*

Lyme disease has been studied only since 1975. In that year it was found in two children living in the town of Lyme in Connecticut, USA. We now know that it occurs in many other parts of the world including Europe and, in Britain, in areas like the New Forest.

It's an interesting disease because the people who get it don't live in poor conditions but in country towns, usually with pleasant gardens and woods nearby! There have been about 1000 cases of Lyme disease in Britain up to now, but in America there are about 15 000 cases every year.

Symptoms

So what happens to you if you get Lyme disease? First, you get an itchy rash; you feel very tired and have a bad headache just like when you have 'flu. After a couple of weeks your heart starts pounding, you get short of breath and you feel dizzy. Then after a few months your joints begin to swell, particularly your knees, which become painful as though you had arthritis. You might also have difficulty remembering things.

Finding the tick

A scientist investigating the disease thought that the clues pointed to the disease being passed to people when they were bitten by an insect or similar animal which crawled rather than flew. (Can you see why he made this deduction?)

Eventually, a patient with the rash remembered being bitten by a **tick** which he had removed from his skin and kept. Ticks are related to spiders, and suck the blood of people or animals. This one was about the size of a pinhead. It was identified as a deer tick, but was it involved in carrying Lyme disease?

The deer tick was much more common in places where Lyme disease occurred than elsewhere; dog ticks, however, are common nearly everywhere. Clearly this was an important finding.

▲ *A red deer tick viewed under a microscope.*

Investigation

When scientists started to study Lyme disease they had to find out two things:

● what caused the disease
● how the disease was passed on to human beings

What would you have done?

Clues

They had a few clues to work on:

● most victims of the disease lived in wooded areas around towns
● the disease wasn't passed on to other members of the family
● most people contracted the disease during the summer months
● it started with a rash which spread from a small spot on the chest or back but not usually on the hands or face

TIVES *at* WORK

Eventually, another scientist looked at the gut contents of deer ticks and found millions of bacteria living there. Some were of a sort which can cause other human diseases. The picture below shows what they looked like.

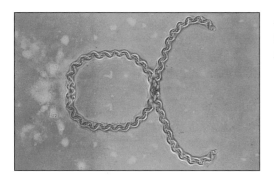

◀ *This type of bacteria is called spirochaetes.*

Next it was found that healthy rabbits could be given Lyme disease by injecting them with a pure culture of this bacterium. At last, now they knew what they were looking for, scientists found the same bacterium in the blood of humans suffering from the disease. So they knew the bacterium was the cause of Lyme disease.

Treatment and eradication

Once a doctor has decided that a patient has got Lyme disease it is fairly easy to treat it using antibiotics like penicillin. It would be better, however, to try to **eradicate** (get rid of) the disease completely. That is easier said than done. Indeed, at the moment, the disease is spreading rapidly in the United States, though fortunately not in Britain. Some of the problems involved in eradicating the disease are as follows:

● one in four deer ticks carry the disease
● there are about 20 000 deer ticks per hectare in the north-eastern United States
● up to 100 larval ticks are found on one mouse
● the deer population in the United States is increasing

How Lyme disease is passed to humans

Humans pick up the ticks when brushing against the undergrowth into which the ticks have climbed to attach themselves to a passing animal.

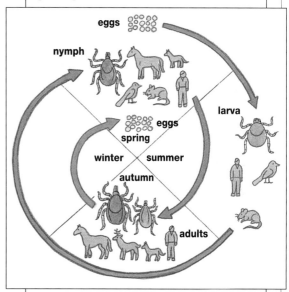

▲ *The life cycle of the red deer tick.*

The following actions have been suggested to fight the disease:

● reduce the deer population
● clear undergrowth in wooded areas where ticks occur
● spray the undergrowth with insecticides
● avoid contact with deer ticks.

How many of these do you think would be worth trying?

Finally, if *you* do go down to the woods some time, take care!

■ *For more about disease detectives see p144–5.*

QUESTIONS

MEASUREMENT

1. The metre used to be defined in terms of the distance between Paris and the North Pole. What is it defined in terms of now?
2. What do the following prefixes mean when used in units; a) mega, b) kilo, c) centi, d) milli?
3. How does a clock based on Caesium compare to one based on quartz for time keeping?

HOW HOT IS IT?

1. What does the temperature of something tell us?
2. What is a thermometric property? Give an example.
3. How could you show that heat and temperature are different things?

KEEPING CLEAN

1. What two substances are the main ingredients of detergents?
2. What advantages do detergents have over soap?
3. What is the advantage of having slightly alkaline toothpaste?

EATING WELL

1. What are the names of the major groups of nutrients?
2. What is malnutrition?

EATING TO YOUR HEART'S CONTENT

1. Where in the world are the highest rates of death from heart disease? Give some possible reasons for this.
2. Give examples of five foods that are high in fat or sugar.

WHAT ARE YOU LIKE INSIDE?

1. How are ultrasound and laser light used in medicine?
2. How is an optical fibre used to remove a blood clot?

MOVEMENT, MUSCLES AND JOINTS

1. What do plants rely on to support themselves?
2. What are three of the key jobs of the skeleton of a mammal?
3. What are antagonistic muscles? Why do they have to work against each other?

HEART AND CIRCULATION

1. Why do we need valves in veins? How do they work?
2. What are capillaries?

EXCRETION: WASTE FROM CELLS

1. What is dialysis?
2. Explain the difference between excretion and egestion.

CELLS AND SPECIALISATION

1. Explain how plant cells are different from animal cells.
2. How is a leaf adapted to photosynthesise?
3. Give an example of two different sorts of animal cells. Explain how they are adapted to do their job.

FRICTION

1. What is friction and what causes it?
2. Give two examples each of when friction is useful and when it is a problem.

ROCKETS AND SATELLITES

1. How do rockets work?
2. Name two different types of satellites. Explain how they orbit the Earth and what they are used for.

NEWTON AND THE MOON

1. What is weight?
2. Give some examples of how Newton put his ideas about gravitation to the test.

FLOATING AND SINKING

1. What is Archimedes' principle?
2. Explain how a submarine dives and resurfaces.
3. What is a hydrometer and what is it used for?
4. Why is the skeleton of a whale small compared to its body size?

BRIDGES

1. What type of forces are produced in a beam bridge when it is loaded?
2. What is special about the forces in an arch bridge?

PLANT ADAPTATIONS

1. How is the cactus adapted to life in the desert?
2. Give two more examples of plants adapted to their surroundings?

PHOTOSYNTHESIS AND FOOD WEBS

1. What is a food web?
2. State three important patterns about food chains and webs.
3. When a cow eats grass, why doesn't all the energy stored in the grass transfer to the cow?
4. What is a pyramid of numbers and a pyramid of biomass?

ENERGY THAT NEVER RUNS OUT

1. What is meant by renewable energy sources?
2. What is geothermal energy?
3. How can tides be used to produce electricity?

NUCLEAR ENERGY

1. What is the difference between fuels like wood and coal and nuclear fuel?
2. Why can radioactive substances be dangerous?

IS IT WORTH IT?

1. What are the two basic methods of getting rid of radioactive waste?
2. Write a report giving the advantages and disadvantages of nuclear power.

WATER ISSUES

1. What is the greenhouse effect?
2. How has the change in the Aral Sea affected the local climate, plant and animal life?

WHAT ARE WE DOING TO OUR WATER?

1. What is eutrophication and how is it caused?
2. Why is the effect of nutrients more dramatic in lakes than rivers?

USING ECHOES

1. What is an echo?
2. What is echolocation and how is it used?

WHAT'S HAPPENING OUT THERE?

1. What is one of the main differences between an insect eye and a human eye?
2. How do bats use echoes?

DARWIN'S VOYAGE

1. What did most scientists think about the Earth, plants and animals in 1831?
2. What were Darwin's observations? Why were these important?

DARWIN'S THEORY OF EVOLUTION

1. What is natural selection?
2. Give an example of natural selection.

WHAT MENDEL DID

1. What is genetics?
2. What did Mendel use in his experiments? What did they show?

FAMILIES THAT ARE DIFFERENT

1. Give an example of a genetic disease.
2. How does a person get a genetic disease?

TEST-TUBE BABIES

1. What do the initials IVF stand for and what do they mean?
2. What is GIFT?
3. List some of the ethical questions that are associated with IVF and GIFT.

WHAT MAKES THEM MOVE?

1. Who first discovered Brownian motion, what was he observing and how did he try to explain it?
2. What are the five key points about Brownian motion?
3. What causes Brownian motion?

THE STORY OF THE ATOM

1. What was Thomson's model of the atom like?
2. How does this compare with today's model?

CHEMICAL REACTIONS AND ENERGY

1. What is meant by the terms exothermic and endothermic reactions? Give an example of each.
2. Where does the energy come from in exothermic reactions?

3. What happens to the mass of the substances that react in a chemical reaction?

ABOUT ACIDS

1. What is the pH scale?
2. What is neutralisation? Give four everyday examples of neutralisation.

GALILEO, KEPLER AND COPERNICUS

1. How were the ideas of Copernicus, Kepler and Galileo different from what everyone else believed at the time?

GALILEO AND HIS TELESCOPE

1. Why did Galileo's book become much better known than either Copernicus's or Kepler's earlier texts?
2. What were the main observations that Galileo made with his telescope?
3. Why do you think the Church leaders of the time reacted badly to Galileo's ideas?

EARTHQUAKES

1. What is a fault?
2. How are earthquakes caused?

VOLCANOES

1. Where do volcanoes form and how do they form?
2. How are the two major types of volcanoes formed?

THE ROCK CYCLE

1. What makes the central core of the Earth hot?
2. Explain how sedimentary, igneous and metamorphic rocks are formed.

THE PERIODIC TABLE

1. What is an element?
2. Describe two of the important patterns in the table.

METALS AND NON METALS

1. List four properties that metals have in common.
2. What is an alloy?
3. What are the two main forms of carbon?

THE EYE AND THE CAMERA

1. How does the eye regulate the amount of light entering it?
2. What is the main difference between the lens in the eye and the lens in the camera?

BEYOND THE RAINBOW

1. How did Newton explain the appearance of a rainbow?
2. What properties do all electromagnetic waves have in common?

COMMUNICATING WITH LIGHT

1. How do optical fibres transmit light?
2. Give some advantages and disadvantages of sending messages along optical fibres compared to sending them along copper wires.

QUESTIONS

LASER LIGHT
1. What does LASER stand for? What is laser light?
2. How are lasers used?

COMPACT DISC
1. How is the information stored on a compact disc?
2. What sort of advantages does a compact disc have over other types of recorded information?

ELECTROSTATICS ALL AROUND
1. What effects do different charges have on each other?
2. Which particles transfer when objects are rubbed together?
3. Give three examples of electrostatics in everyday life.

APPLICATIONS OF ELECTROSTATICS
1. Explain how electrostatics is used to extract pollution from power stations, and how it is used in the photocopier.

THUNDER AND LIGHTNING
1. Why do you notice the thunder after the lightning if you are several kilometres away from a thunder storm?
2. How does a lightning conductor work?

WHAT IS ELECTRICITY?
1. What are the names of the three particles that make up all atoms (except hydrogen)?
2. How does electricity cause the water in a kettle to heat up?

MAGNETS AND MAGNETISM
1. Describe how you could make a piece of steel into a magnet.
2. What is a domain? What is the difference between the domains in a magnet and the domains in an unmagnetised piece of steel?
3. How can a steel bar be magnetised by hammering?
4. What type of compass does not rely on magnetism?

MICHAEL FARADAY
1. What is the link between electricity and magnetism?
2. Describe one of Faraday's most famous experiments.

THE ELECTRIC MOTOR
1. Give five examples of things which rely on an electric motor for their operation.
2. What is the basic principle of an electric motor?

GENERATING ELECTRICITY
1. What are the main components of a bike dynamo? How does it generate electricity?
2. Explain how a power station generates electricity.

TRANSFORMERS
1. Give three examples of devices that contain a transformer. What does a transformer do?
2. Why are transformers used in the National Grid?

RAW MATERIALS
1. What is a raw material? Give examples of five products and their raw materials.
2. What is a mineral?

PURE MATERIALS AND MIXTURES
1. What do scientists mean by a pure substance?
2. List the five main types of mixture and give an example of each.
3. How do scientists decide if a material is pure?

MATERIALS IN THE HOME
1. Give five examples of different materials used in house construction.
2. What sort of factors are used to decide which materials should be used?
3. Give three advantages of plastic as a material for guttering.

PESTICIDES AND INSECTICIDES
1. Give an advantage and a disadvantage of using pesticides.
2. How does an insecticide like DDT end up in a peregrine falcon?
3. Give three reasons why people prefer to use fewer chemicals in farming.

A NATURAL INSECTICIDE
1. What are natural insecticides based on?
2. What is biological pest control?

DRUGS AND MEDICINES
1. What is a drug? What is the difference between a drug and a medicine?
2. What is a synthetic drug?

BACTERIA AND VIRUSES
1. Name two diseases caused by (i) a bacteria (ii) a virus.
2. Describe how the body is able to defend itself from invading bacteria.

NEW DISEASES
1. Name three 'new diseases'. Where do 'new diseases' come from?
2. How is the HIV thought to affect the body?
3. Describe how the body produces antibodies.
4. Explain the term 'immunisation'.

ANTIBIOTICS
1. What are antibiotics?
2. Why should we be very careful with our use of antibiotics?

DISEASE DETECTIVES AT WORK
1. What causes Lyme Disease?
2. Why is it difficult to get rid of Lyme Disease?
3. What suggestions have been made to fight the disease?

INDEX